Better Homes and Gardens®
AMERICA's ETHNIC CUISINES

Better Homes and Gardens® Books
Des Moines, Iowa

Better Homes and Gardens® Books
An imprint of Meredith® Books

America's Ethnic Cuisines

Editor: Chuck Smothermon
Contributing Editor: Margaret Smith
Senior Associate Design Director: Doug Samuelson
Copy Chief: Terri Fredrickson
Copy and Production Editor: Victoria Forlini
Editorial Operations Manager: Karen Schirm
Managers, Book Production: Pam Kvitne, Marjorie J. Schenkelberg,
  Rick von Holdt
Contributing Copy Editor: Kim Catanzarite
Contributing Proofreaders: Susie Kling, Elise Marton,
  Gretchen Kauffman
Photographer: Jay Wilde
Contributing Photographers: Marty Baldwin, Ken Carlson
Prop Stylist: Susan Strelecki
Contributing Writers: Lisa Kingsley, Lisa Holderness
Recipe Developers: Ellen Boeke, Lori Powell Gordon,
  Shelli McConnell, Carlo and Jonna Paglicci
Food Stylists: Charles Worthington, Dianna Nolin
Electronic Production Coordinator: Paula Forest
Editorial and Design Assistants: Karen McFadden, Mary Lee Gavin
Test Kitchen Director: Lynn Blanchard
Test Kitchen Product Supervisor: Marilyn Cornelius
Test Kitchen Home Economists: Juliana Hale; Laura Harms, R.D.;
  Jennifer Kalinowski, R.D.; Maryellyn Krantz; Jill Moberly;
  Colleen Weeden; Lori Wilson

Meredith® Books

Editor in Chief: Linda Raglan Cunningham
Design Director: Matt Strelecki
Executive Editor, Food and Crafts: Jennifer Dorland Darling

Publisher: James D. Blume
Executive Director, Marketing: Jeffrey Myers
Executive Director, New Business Development: Todd M. Davis
Executive Director, Sales: Ken Zagor
Director, Operations: George A. Susral
Director, Production: Douglas M. Johnston
Business Director: Jim Leonard

Vice President and General Manager: Douglas J. Guendel

Better Homes and Gardens® Magazine

Editor in Chief: Karol DeWulf Nickell
Deputy Editor, Food and Entertaining: Nancy Hopkins

Meredith Publishing Group

President, Publishing Group: Stephen M. Lacy
Vice President-Publishing Director: Bob Mate

Meredith Corporation

Chairman and Chief Executive Officer: William T. Kerr

In Memoriam: E. T. Meredith III (1933–2003)

All of us at Better Homes and Gardens®
Books are dedicated to providing you with
the information and ideas you need to
create delicious foods. We welcome your
comments and suggestions. Write to us at:
Better Homes and Gardens Books,
Cookbook Editorial Department, 1716
Locust St., Des Moines, IA 50309-3023.

If you would like to purchase any of our
cooking, crafts, gardening, home
improvement, or home decorating and
design books, check wherever quality books
are sold. Or visit us at: bhgbooks.com

Our seal assures you that every recipe in
America's Ethnic Cuisines has been tested in
the Better Homes and Gardens® Test
Kitchen. This means that each recipe is
practical and reliable, and meets our high
standards of taste appeal. We guarantee
your satisfaction with this book for as long
as you own it.

Additional Photography:

CORBIS: Kevin R. Morris p. 8, second row left, second
row right / Karen Huntt Mason p. 56, first row left /
Owen Franken p. 56, third row left / Michael Freeman p. 160,
first row left / Robert Semeniuk p. 160, second row right /
Martin Jones p. 160, third row center / David Cumming
p. 190, first row left / Ron Watts p. 190, third row right /
Gail Mooney p. 216, first row right / Dave Bartruff p. 216,
second row left / Michelle Garrett p. 216, third row left

Getty Images: Bob Thomas p. 192 / Victoria Pearson
p. 216, first row left

Homemade Fettucine with Arugula, Tomato, and Olive Sauce, page 64

Contents

5

INTRODUCTION

The broad diversity of culture that makes up America's melting pot has added much to Americans' everyday lives. And for diners and cooks in particular, it has brought an amazing variety of wonderful things to eat! Through its authentic recipes, gorgeous photographs, cooking history, tradition, instruction, and lore, *America's Ethnic Cuisines* is a celebration of the glorious food contributed to America by its invaluable immigrant population.

What are America's ethnic cuisines?

A multitude of ethnic groups in America have contributed greatly to the way this country eats. Unfortunately, it is impossible to give them all their due in a work of this size and scope. Thus, in an effort to provide meaningful insight to several, the focus has been narrowed to seven of the most popular cuisines in America, including Asian, Italian, Mexican, Indian, Caribbean, Mediterranean/Middle Eastern, and Cajun/Creole. The diversity of flavors, ingredients, and cooking styles represented by these seven cuisines provides a great view—and taste—of some of the best food this country has to offer.

The recipes

With the help and guidance of the Better Homes and Gardens® Test Kitchen, an extraordinary collection of recipes was assembled and tested that reflect how ethnic dishes and meals are prepared in America—that is, in American kitchens and with ingredients that are available throughout America. This approach makes it easier than ever for home cooks to experience the true flavor of each style of cooking and to share their findings in authentic meals for family and friends. Better yet, this book showcases these dishes as they are most apt to be served across the country. In other words, *America's Ethnic Cuisines* is about the way Americans of all backgrounds eat here today, lending a unique perspective to the reader and cook.

As always, Better Homes and Gardens'® recipes are written clearly and concisely, in a no-nonsense manner that ensures your success. You'll find preparation and cook times and nutrition information with each recipe, and detailed how-to photos and instructions accompany several key recipes. Numerous beautiful, full-color photographs of the finished recipes inspire and enlighten.

How the book is organized

Each chapter begins with an overview of a particular type of cooking, followed by photos and background information on some of the key ingredients of that cuisine. You'll learn the history and practical information that will make your cooking better and more fun. And with so many ingredient photos as a guide, you won't be mystified the next time you shop for a new ingredient you'd like to try.

To eliminate the guesswork and make it easy for you to serve entire ethnic meals, every one of the more than 150 recipes in *America's Ethnic Cuisines* is presented as part of a menu. Follow the suggestions or put together your own menus, mixing and matching favorite recipes.

Start cooking—or perhaps not!

Many cookbooks are meant only for the kitchen, others mainly for the armchair. This book is meant for both. With engaging history, practical cooking information, gorgeous photographs, and amazing recipes, *America's Ethnic Cuisines* is a rare cookbook that is beautiful to look at and read and to take into the kitchen and cook from too.

MULBERRY MEAT MARKET

Appetizers

Asian Pickled Carrots   21
Cabbage- and Pork-Filled Baked Buns   40
Egg Rolls   36
Fresh Spring Rolls   16
Teriyaki Beef and Lettuce Wraps   51

Soups & Salads

Asian Chicken Noodle Soup   33
Hot and Sour Soup   39
Mushroom, Noodle, and Tofu Soup   45
Peanut Soup   27
Thai Chicken Coconut Soup   15
Thai Noodle Salad   28
Wonton Soup   53

Asian

9

Entrées

Cantonese Spareribs   24
Cashew Pork and Broccoli   42
Chicken Pad Thai   48
Garlic Chicken   30
Green Curry Chicken   47
Mu Shu Pork   43
Sesame Chicken and Vegetables   23
Soy-Ginger Salmon   18
Szechuan Shrimp   35
Vegetable Fried Rice   54

Desserts

Almond Cake with Fresh Fruit   31
Banana Wontons   55
Ginger Custard   49
Homemade Fortune Cookies   25
Sweet Sticky Rice with Mango   19
Vanilla Pear Ice Cream   37

The fact that several American cities—San Francisco, New York, and Chicago among them—have for many years maintained bustling and vibrant areas called Chinatown says something about the strength of Asian culture. Those who live in these places can take in the Chinese atmosphere at a moment's notice, and that means shopping and, of course, eating. The appeal of Asian food is so widespread that even this country's smallest Midwestern meat-and-potatoes towns have a much-loved Chinese restaurant that is frequented by the locals.

The Chinese began immigrating to the United States in the mid-19th century. By 1880, 25 percent of the workforce in California was of Chinese descent. Chop suey and chow mein have been part of America's culinary vernacular since then. It wasn't until the late 1970s, though, after the Vietnam War ended and thousands of Vietnamese immigrants came to North America to start a new life, that Americans became acquainted with the exquisite foods of Southeast Asia. In the decade that followed, interest in Asian foods of every type grew as hot as a searing Szechwan pepper. Woks began selling like those proverbial hotcakes.

Today Americans are as likely (or maybe even more likely) to get a hankering for a steaming bowl of Thai coconut soup or a pyramid of crisp, cool Vietnamese-style spring rolls as they are for mashed potatoes and gravy.

The techniques used for all types of Asian cooking are similar: stir-frying, steaming, stewing (as in a curry), and barbecue. It is the combination of the common ingredients and how they're prepared that earmarks a dish Chinese, Vietnamese, or Thai. Learn a few basic techniques and you'll be rewarded with a host of new and delicious dishes.

ginger, crystallized ginger

shiitake mushrooms

napa cabbage

clockwise, from upper left: somen, yamagata somen, rice vermicelli, chinese bean threads, vermicelli bean threads

rice, wheat, and udon noodles

lemongrass

baby bok choy

short grain, sticky, and jasmine rice

Asian cooking involves a variety of ingredients almost as vast as the geographic area Asia encompasses. Vegetables such as Chinese cabbages, bamboo shoots, water chestnuts, and lemongrass are virtually unique to Asian cooking, while Asian staples such as rice, mushrooms, ginger, carrots, and noodles are—or have become—important parts of other cuisines. A few of the most significant ingredients include the following.

Ginger is a spicy and aromatic flavoring that originated in Southeast Asia. The edible portion of ginger comes from its rhizome, an underground root-like section. (This is why it is often called gingerroot.) Despite its Asian origins, much ginger is now grown in Jamaica, and the charm of its flavor has spread to many cuisines, including those of Europe.

Chinese cabbages are important ingredients in many Asian dishes. Bok choy, in particular, is a popular variety with an appealing flavor and texture. With cooking, its leaves wilt while the stalks remain slightly crunchy.

While certainly not unique to Asian cooking, mushrooms are nonetheless essential to many dishes. **Shiitake** is a key variety with an almost meaty texture and flavor. Its cap is the only part that is eaten, but the woody stems can be boiled to add depth of flavor to soups and broths.

Noodles are today a major component of several world cuisines and have been important to Asian cooking for many centuries. There is a tremendous variety of noodles used in the cuisines of the region, but one important feature for cooks to consider is that Asian noodles are made from several different ingredients, including rice flour, several types of wheat flour, and soy- and mung-bean starch. Familiarity with the flavor and texture of noodles made from specific flours and starches gives cooks clues as to what they may expect when cooking new varieties. Many of these noodles are available in both fresh and dried versions.

Rice is a dietary staple for approximately half the world's people, and it would be difficult to overstate its importance to global cooking. It is central to Asian cooking. In Asia, as a broad generalization, short grain rice is preferred in Japanese cooking, while long grain varieties are preferred on the continent. Different varieties of rice have differing starch qualities, and this helps determine how each variety is used by cooks. Glutinous, or sticky rice, for instance, has a large proportion of a type of starch that causes it to cling tightly together. This makes it ideal for thick, sticky rice desserts (see recipe, page 19). As a side dish, however, this intensely sticky quality does not partner as well with many dishes as a less sticky rice might. Finally, some varieties of rice are distinguished by their fragrance or distinctive flavor. An example is jasmine rice from Thailand.

THAI CHICKEN COCONUT SOUP

In its many slightly different incarnations, this classic soup—called *kai tom kah* in Thai—is always a little bit sweet, a little bit hot, and deeply satisfying. A cup makes a nice starter; a bowl is a full meal.

Start to Finish: 25 minutes   **Makes:** 4 to 5 servings

3 cups chicken broth

2 tablespoons fresh lime juice

1 tablespoon fish sauce (nuoc nam or nam pla*) or ½ teaspoon anchovy paste

4 thin slices fresh ginger

1 pound boneless, skinless chicken thighs, trimmed and cut into ¼-inch strips

½ cup unsweetened coconut milk*

⅛ teaspoon red pepper flakes

4 ounces pea pods, trimmed, and halved, if large

½ cup shredded carrots

¼ cup chopped fresh cilantro

2 cups hot cooked rice

1 In a large saucepan bring chicken broth, lime juice, fish sauce, and ginger to boiling; reduce heat and simmer for 3 minutes.

2 Add chicken, coconut milk, and red pepper flakes. Return to boiling; simmer, covered, for 4 minutes or until chicken is no longer pink.

3 Add pea pods and carrots; cook for 1 minute or until peas are crisp-tender. Stir in cilantro. Serve in soup bowls with cooked rice.

*Note: Fish sauce and coconut milk are available in Asian markets and specialty sections of supermarkets.

Nutrition Facts per serving: 347 cal., 11 g total fat (6 g sat. fat), 90 mg chol., 1,193 mg sodium, 28 g carbo., 1 g fiber, 28 g pro. **Daily Values:** 92% vit. A, 22% vit. C, 5% calcium, 16% iron

FRESH SPRING ROLLS

The rice-paper wrappers used to make these Vietnamese-style spring rolls may start out brittle, but in the end they're soft and pliable. Never fried, the shrimp and vegetable rolls are an exquisitely light way to start an Asian feast.

Start to Finish: 50 minutes   **Makes:** 24 rolls

2 ounces dried rice vermicelli noodles
24 medium shrimp, peeled and deveined
2 cups shredded napa cabbage
1 cup shredded carrots
½ cup fresh cilantro leaves
½ cup fresh mint leaves or flat-leaf parsley
24 round rice-paper wrappers (8½-inch diameter)

½ cup water
2 tablespoons sugar
2 tablespoons rice wine vinegar
1 tablespoon fish sauce (nuoc nam or nam pla*)
1 tablespoon finely shredded carrot

1 In a medium saucepan cook the vermicelli in lightly salted boiling water for 3 minutes; drain. Rinse under cold water; drain well. Use kitchen shears to snip the noodles into small pieces; set aside.

2 In a large saucepan cook the shrimp in lightly salted boiling water for 1 to 2 minutes or until opaque; drain. Rinse with cold water; drain again. Halve the shrimp lengthwise; set aside.

3 In a large bowl combine cooked vermicelli, cabbage, the 1 cup shredded carrots, cilantro, and mint leaves; set aside.

4 Pour 1 cup warm water into a shallow dish. Dip rice papers, one at a time, into water; gently shake off excess water. Place the wet rice papers between clean, damp, 100-percent-cotton kitchen towels; let stand for 10 minutes. Brush any dry edges with a little additional water. Place a well-rounded tablespoon of cabbage mixture across lower third of 1 softened rice paper (keep others covered). Fold bottom of rice paper over filling; arrange 2 shrimp halves across filling; fold in paper sides. Tightly roll up the rice paper and filling. Place, seam side down, on a large plate. Repeat with remaining rice paper, filling, and shrimp. Cover and chill for up to 6 hours.

5 For dipping sauce, in a small saucepan combine the ½ cup water and the sugar. Bring to boiling over medium heat, stirring occasionally, until sugar is dissolved. Remove from heat and stir in rice wine vinegar, fish sauce, and the 1 tablespoon shredded carrot. Serve spring rolls with dipping sauce.

*Note: Find fish sauce in Asian markets and specialty sections of supermarkets.

Nutrition Facts per roll: 65 cal., 0 g total fat (0 g sat. fat), 10 mg chol., 55 mg sodium, 13 g carbo., 1 g fiber, 2 g pro.
Daily Values: 33% vit. A, 9% vit. C, 2% calcium, 5% iron

16

After soaking in warm water, rice paper becomes pliable.

Add filling and fold over one side of the rice paper. Place shrimp on top; fold in sides.

Finally, tightly roll up the filling and rice paper. Place the spring rolls seam side down to serve.

SOY-GINGER SALMON

Truly a fusion of influences and flavors, this Asian-style dish features a fish farmed in the cold waters of Canada, Alaska, and Norway. Other unexpected ingredients include tiny Italian pasta (orzo) and fresh spinach.

Start to Finish: 35 minutes   **Makes:** 4 servings

- 3 tablespoons soy sauce
- 2 tablespoons water
- 1 tablespoon sugar
- ½ teaspoon grated fresh ginger
- 1 pound salmon fillet, skinned and cut into 4 pieces
- ½ teaspoon sesame seeds
- 2 teaspoons cooking oil
- Nonstick cooking spray

- 1 clove garlic, minced (or ½ teaspoon bottled minced garlic)
- 3 10-ounce bags fresh spinach, stems removed
- 2 tablespoons water
- ½ teaspoon salt
- ¼ teaspoon toasted sesame oil
- 2 cups cooked orzo
- 4 green onions, sliced

1 Combine soy sauce, 2 tablespoons water, sugar, and ginger in a baking dish. Add salmon, turning to coat; let stand for 15 minutes.

2 Meanwhile, heat a large nonstick skillet over medium heat for 1 minute. Add sesame seeds. Toast seeds for 2½ to 3 minutes; remove from skillet. Drain salmon, reserving marinade.

3 Add cooking oil to the skillet and heat for 1 minute over medium-high heat. Add salmon, skin side up; cook for 3 to 4 minutes. Reduce heat to medium; turn salmon, cover and cook for 3 minutes more or until fish flakes easily with a fork. Transfer salmon to serving plate. Add reserved marinade to skillet and boil for 1 to 2 minutes or until syrupy.

4 Meanwhile, lightly coat a Dutch oven with cooking spray. Heat for 1 minute over medium heat. Add garlic, spinach, and 2 tablespoons water. Cover and cook for 3 to 4 minutes or until spinach is wilted, stirring occasionally. Stir in salt and sesame oil. Serve salmon, topped with soy glaze and sesame seeds, with spinach and orzo. Garnish with green onions.

Nutrition Facts per serving: 355 cal., 14 g total fat (2 g sat. fat), 69 mg chol., 1,289 mg sodium, 24 g carbo., 19 g fiber, 35 g pro. **Daily Values:** 230% vit. A, 88% vit. C, 19% calcium, 89% iron

SWEET STICKY RICE WITH MANGO

Although Asians are not big dessert eaters, the American indulgence in something sweet after a meal has made this rice dish a regular on many Thai restaurant menus. If you'd like to serve it in a pretty molded shape, divide the rice among four 6-ounce custard cups, press lightly, and unmold onto plates.

Prep: 15 minutes plus 4 hours soaking time   **Cook:** 25 minutes   **Stand:** 30 minutes   **Makes:** 4 servings

1¼ cups sticky rice, glutinous rice, or sweet rice*

1 cup purchased unsweetened coconut milk

⅓ cup packed brown sugar

¼ teaspoon salt

¼ teaspoon rose water (optional)

2 fresh mangoes, seeded, peeled, and sliced

1 In a large bowl combine rice and enough room-temperature water to cover. Cover and let rice soak for 4 to 24 hours. Drain and rinse rice.

2 Line a steamer basket with a wet double thickness of 100-percent-cotton cheesecloth. Place steamer basket in a saucepan. Add water to just below the bottom of steamer basket. Spread rice evenly onto cheesecloth in steamer basket. Bring to boiling; reduce heat. Cover and steam about 25 minutes or until rice is shiny and tender. Do not let water completely evaporate; add more hot water, if necessary. Transfer rice to a large bowl.

3 In a small saucepan heat and stir coconut milk, brown sugar, and salt over medium heat until hot, but not boiling, and sugar is dissolved. Remove from heat. If desired, stir in rose water. Pour hot coconut milk mixture over rice. Stir to combine. Let stand for 30 minutes to blend flavors.

4 To serve, spoon warm rice into center of four dessert plates (or spoon one-fourth of the rice into a small bowl, press lightly, and unmold onto dessert plate). Arrange mango slices around rice.

*Note: Sticky rice, a medium to long grain rice, is a cooking staple in northern Thailand. Because it is very low in amylose and high in amylopectin (components of starch), cooking results in a sticky, yet not mushy, texture. It is available at Southeast Asian markets and large supermarkets or by mail order.

Nutrition Facts per serving: 474 cal., 11 g total fat (10 g sat. fat), 0 mg chol., 171 mg sodium, 88 g carbo., 2 g fiber, 5 g pro. **Daily Values:** 81% vit. A, 48% vit. C, 3% calcium, 9% iron

~~ Menu ~~

Asian Pickled Carrots

Sesame Chicken & Vegetables

Cantonese Spareribs

Homemade fortune cookies

ASIAN PICKLED CARROTS

Serve these spiced sweet-sour carrots as an appetizer or as a cold, crisp accompaniment to hot foods.

Start to Finish: 45 minutes   **Makes:** 3 half-pint jars (about 6 appetizer servings per half-pint)

1 **16-ounce bag baby carrots**
1 **teaspoon salt**
¼ **cup peeled fresh ginger, cut into thin strips**
3 **whole allspice**

¾ **cup water**
¾ **cup rice vinegar**
⅓ **cup packed brown sugar**
4 **whole cloves**
4 **whole peppercorns**

1 In a medium saucepan cook carrots and salt, covered, in a small amount of boiling water for 3 minutes or until crisp-tender. Drain; place in 3 clean half-pint jars. Place some of the fresh ginger and 1 whole allspice in each jar.

2 In a medium saucepan combine water, vinegar, brown sugar, cloves, and peppercorns. Bring mixture to boiling; reduce heat and simmer, uncovered, for 5 minutes. Pour over carrots. Seal jars and refrigerate for up to 3 months.

Nutrition Facts per appetizer serving: 32 cal., 0 g total fat (0 g sat. fat), 0 mg chol., 140 mg sodium, 7 g carbo., 1 g fiber, 0 g pro. **Daily Values:** 128% vit. A, 3% vit. C, 1% calcium, 1% iron

SESAME CHICKEN AND VEGETABLES

Two kinds of sesame oil are available: a light version that gives stir-fries just a hint of extra flavor and a darker, more fragrant version that is used as an intense flavor booster. Use the lighter type for this quick Chinese chicken and vegetable dish.

Prep: 30 minutes   **Marinate:** 1 hour   **Cook:** 10 minutes   **Makes:** 4 servings

12 ounces skinless, boneless chicken breasts	1 tablespoon light sesame oil
2 tablespoons soy sauce	1½ cups thinly bias-sliced carrots
2 tablespoons chicken broth	1 cup jicama cut into thin, bite-size strips
2 tablespoons chopped green onion	2 cups fresh medium pea pods, strings removed, or one 6-ounce package frozen pea pods
1 tablespoon snipped fresh parsley	
1 tablespoon rice vinegar	
1½ teaspoons sesame seeds	2 cups hot cooked brown rice
1 clove garlic, minced	Sesame seeds, toasted (optional)
1½ teaspoons grated fresh ginger	

1 Cut chicken into bite-size strips. For marinade, in a shallow nonmetallic dish combine soy sauce, chicken broth, green onion, parsley, rice vinegar, the 1½ teaspoons sesame seeds, garlic, and ginger. Add chicken to marinade, stirring to coat. Cover and chill for 1 hour.

2 Add the 1 tablespoon sesame oil to a wok or 12-inch skillet. Preheat over medium-high heat (add more oil as necessary during cooking). Stir-fry carrots in hot oil for 1 minute. Add jicama and fresh pea pods (if using); stir-fry about 2 to 3 minutes more or until crisp-tender. Remove vegetables from wok. Drain chicken, reserving marinade. Add chicken to wok; stir-fry for 2 to 3 minutes or until no longer pink. Push chicken from center of wok.

3 Add reserved marinade to center of wok. Cook and stir until bubbly. Return cooked vegetables to wok. Add frozen pea pods (if using). Stir to coat. Cook and stir about 1 minute more or until heated through. Serve immediately over hot cooked brown rice, spooning sauce over top. If desired, garnish with toasted sesame seeds.

Nutrition Facts per serving: 315 cal., 6 g total fat (1 g sat. fat), 49 mg chol., 565 mg sodium, 34 g carbo., 4 g fiber, 25 g pro. **Daily Values:** 260% vit. A, 29% vit. C, 6% calcium, 12% iron

23

CANTONESE SPARERIBS

The port city of Canton, located in the south of China, is famous for roasted meats such as these succulent sweet-and-tangy pork ribs. Serve them with steamed rice and vegetables.

Prep: 10 minutes   **Roast:** 2 hours   **Oven:** 450°F/350°F   **Makes:** 4 servings

- 4 **pounds meaty pork spareribs or pork loin back ribs, cut into serving pieces**
- 1 **cup orange marmalade**
- ¾ **cup water**
- ⅓ **cup reduced-sodium soy sauce**
- 2 **cloves garlic, minced, or ½ teaspoon garlic powder**

- ½ **teaspoon ground ginger**
- **Dash black pepper**
- **Orange wedges (optional)**
- **Green onion brushes (optional)**

1 Place ribs, meaty side down, in a shallow roasting pan. Roast, uncovered, in a 450° oven for 30 minutes. Remove from oven; carefully drain fat from ribs.

2 Turn ribs meaty side up. Reduce oven temperature to 350°; continue roasting ribs, uncovered, for 1 hour. Carefully drain off fat. In a medium bowl combine the marmalade, water, soy sauce, garlic, ginger, and pepper; stir thoroughly. Pour over the ribs.

3 Roast ribs, uncovered, for 30 minutes more or until tender, spooning sauce over ribs occasionally. If desired, serve with orange wedges and garnish with green onion brushes.

Nutrition Facts per serving: 915 cal., 53 g total fat (19 g sat. fat), 214 mg chol., 969 mg sodium, 55 g carbo., 0 g fiber, 53 g pro. **Daily Values:** 2% vit. A, 9% vit. C, 13% calcium, 21% iron

24

HOMEMADE FORTUNE COOKIES

Bring out your inner scribe: Write personalized predictions for the fortunate family and friends who get to eat these fun and tasty treats.

Prep: 1 hour 15 minutes plus decorating   **Bake:** 4 minutes per batch   **Stand:** 1 hour   **Oven:** 400°F
Makes: about 2 dozen cookies

2 **egg whites**
½ **cup superfine sugar**
½ **cup all-purpose flour**
1 **tablespoon butter (no substitutes)**
¼ **teaspoon salt**
¼ **teaspoon vanilla**
¼ **teaspoon almond extract**

Red and green construction paper
Silver and gold felt-tip pens (nonglitter)
3 **ounces semisweet chocolate, melted and cooled**
3 **ounces white baking bar, melted and cooled**

1 Let egg whites stand at room temperature for 30 minutes. Grease 2 large nonstick baking sheets. In a medium bowl vigorously whisk egg whites, sugar, flour, butter, salt, vanilla, and almond extract until smooth. Let batter stand for 10 minutes.

2 Meanwhile, cut paper into twenty-four 3×½-inch strips. Write fortunes on strips with pens.

3 To bake 2 cookies per sheet, dip the rim of a 3¼-inch diameter glass into the batter. Gently press the glass onto a prepared baking sheet to mark a circle. Trace a second circle 5 inches from the first. Spoon 1 heaping teaspoon of batter into the center of each circle. Spread batter evenly with back of spoon to fill the circle. Bake in a 400° oven, one sheet at a time, for 4 to 5 minutes or until cookie edges are brown (they may brown unevenly, which is OK).

4 Transfer baking sheet to a rack. Working very quickly, remove 1 cookie with a thin, flexible metal spatula and place it bottom side up on work surface. Place a paper fortune strip on center of cookie, extending one end of paper from one side. Fold cookie in half; place the folded edge against the rim of a glass measure. Press the ends down, holding the cookie in place for about 10 seconds or until it begins to harden. Repeat for the second cookie (if it becomes too hard to shape, return it to the oven for a few seconds to soften). Cool cookies on a wire rack. Repeat with remaining batter, cleaning, drying, and greasing baking sheets after each batch.

5 Dip the cookie halves without the protruding paper fortunes into melted semisweet chocolate or white chocolate. Transfer to wire racks. Let cookies stand 1 hour until set.

Nutrition Facts per cookie: 68 cal., 2 g total fat (2 g sat. fat), 2 mg chol., 37 mg sodium, 10 g carbo., 0 g fiber, 1 g pro.
Daily Values: 1% calcium, 2% iron

MENU

Peanut Soup

Thai Noodle Salad

Garlic Chicken

Almond Cake
with Fresh Fruit

PEANUT SOUP

Want to cook up some Thai flavors fast? This creamy, peanutty soup goes together in less than 30 minutes and satisfies your craving with the sweet and savory flavors of coconut milk, lemongrass, and ground red pepper.

Start to Finish: 30 minutes   **Makes:** 4 servings

⅓ **cup finely chopped onion**

⅓ **cup finely chopped celery**

½ **cup finely chopped red sweet pepper**

1 **tablespoon butter**

1 **tablespoon all-purpose flour**

1 **tablespoon very finely chopped lemongrass (white portion only) or 1 teaspoon finely shredded lemon peel**

¼ **teaspoon cayenne pepper**

1 **14-ounce can vegetable broth**

1 **13½-ounce can unsweetened coconut milk**

¼ **cup creamy peanut butter**

1 **tablespoon soy sauce**

Chopped peanuts (optional)

Snipped fresh cilantro (optional)

1 In a 2-quart saucepan cook onion, celery, and ¼ cup of the red sweet pepper in hot butter over medium heat about 5 minutes or until vegetables are tender, stirring occasionally. Stir in the flour, lemongrass, and ground red pepper. Add broth and coconut milk all at once. Cook and stir until the mixture is slightly thickened and bubbly. Cook and stir for 1 minute more. (Mixture may look curdled.)

2 Stir peanut butter and soy sauce into mixture in saucepan; cook and stir until well mixed and heated through. To serve, ladle soup into bowls. Top with remaining chopped red sweet pepper and, if desired, peanuts and cilantro.

Nutrition Facts per serving: 327 cal., 29 g total fat (20 g sat. fat), 8 mg chol., 780 mg sodium, 12 g carbo., 2 g fiber, 7 g pro. **Daily Values:** 26% vit. A, 52% vit. C, 2% calcium, 8% iron

THAI NOODLE SALAD

Delicate vermicelli, crunchy vegetables, and shredded roasted chicken wear a coat of creamy peanut sauce in this main-dish salad that inspires patio dining.

Start to Finish: 35 minutes   **Makes:** 4 servings

  6 ounces dried vermicelli or thin spaghetti
  ¼ cup soy sauce
  ¼ cup chicken or vegetable broth
  2 tablespoons peanut butter
  1 tablespoon fresh lime juice
  1 teaspoon minced garlic
  1 teaspoon grated fresh ginger
     or ½ teaspoon ground ginger
  ½ teaspoon crushed red pepper

  1½ cups shredded or chopped cooked rotisserie chicken or turkey breast
  1 red sweet pepper, cut into thin bite-size pieces
  3 green onions, bias-sliced into ½-inch pieces
  ¼ cup snipped fresh cilantro
     Lime wedges
  2 tablespoons finely chopped peanuts (optional)

1 Cook vermicelli according to package directions; drain.

2 Meanwhile, in a saucepan combine soy sauce, broth, peanut butter, lime juice, garlic, ginger, and crushed red pepper. Cook and stir over low heat until peanut butter is melted. Add cooked pasta; toss to coat.

3 Add chicken, sweet pepper, green onions, and cilantro; mix well. Serve warm or let stand at room temperature for up to 30 minutes. Serve with lime wedges. If desired, garnish with peanuts.

Nutrition Facts per serving: 334 cal., 8 g total fat (2 g sat. fat), 46 mg chol., 1,071 mg sodium, 37 g carbo., 2 g fiber, 25 g pro. **Daily Values:** 40% vit. A, 109% vit. C, 4% calcium, 14% iron

GARLIC CHICKEN

No take-home boxes needed (you're already home!) when you stir up this classic Chinese restaurant dish. Serve it with a pot of hot oolong tea and some fortune cookies and you won't even miss dining out.

Prep: 20 minutes   **Marinate:** 30 minutes   **Cook:** 6 minutes   **Makes:** 4 servings

12 ounces skinless, boneless chicken breasts

1 cup water

3 tablespoons reduced-sodium soy sauce

2 tablespoons dry white wine or water

1 tablespoon cornstarch

2 tablespoons cooking oil

10 green onions, bias-sliced into 1-inch pieces

1 cup thinly sliced fresh mushrooms

12 cloves garlic, peeled and finely chopped, or 2 tablespoons bottled minced garlic

½ cup sliced water chestnuts

Hot cooked white rice, jasmine rice, or basmati rice (optional)

1 Cut chicken into ½-inch pieces. Place chicken in a plastic bag set in a shallow bowl.

2 For marinade, combine water, soy sauce, and white wine; pour marinade over chicken in bag. Marinate in the refrigerator for 30 minutes. Drain chicken, reserving the marinade. Stir cornstarch into the reserved marinade; set aside.

3 Pour oil into a wok or large skillet. (Add more oil as necessary during cooking.) Heat over medium-high heat. Cook and stir green onions, mushrooms, and garlic in hot oil for 1 to 2 minutes or until tender. Remove vegetables from wok. Add chicken to wok. Cook and stir for 2 to 3 minutes or until no longer pink. Push chicken from center of wok. Stir marinade mixture; add to center of wok. Cook and stir until thickened and bubbly.

4 Return cooked vegetables to wok. Add water chestnuts. Cook and stir about 1 minute more or until heated through. If desired, serve with hot cooked rice.

Nutrition Facts per serving: 226 cal., 9 g total fat (1 g sat. fat), 49 mg chol., 491 mg sodium, 13 g carbo., 2 g fiber, 23 g pro. **Daily Values:** 4% vit. A, 19% vit. C, 6% calcium, 10% iron

Garlic Chicken Stir-Fry with Cashews: Prepare as above, except stir ½ teaspoon crushed red pepper into marinade mixture. Stir in 1 cup cashews with water chestnuts.

Nutrition Facts per serving: 422 cal., 25 g total fat (5 g sat. fat), 49 mg chol., 497 mg sodium, 25 g carbo., 3 g fiber, 28 g pro. **Daily Values:** 5% vit. A, 19% vit. C, 8% calcium, 22% iron

ALMOND CAKE WITH FRESH FRUIT

In a word, this rich, orange-flavored nut cake is heavenly—and so is its symbolism. Fresh oranges, traditionally served as a wish for good fortune during the Chinese New Year, are believed to resemble a particular fruit found in paradise.

Prep: 20 minutes   **Bake:** 20 minutes   **Cool:** 1 hour   **Oven:** 350°F   **Makes:** 8 servings

1 tablespoon all-purpose flour

½ teaspoon baking powder

½ teaspoon finely shredded orange peel

2 eggs

⅓ cup sugar

6 ounces whole unblanched almonds

¼ cup orange juice

¼ cup orange liqueur or orange juice

½ cup thinly sliced dried papaya and/or persimmon

2 medium pears, quartered and, if desired, cored

½ cup seedless green grapes and/or orange or grapefruit sections

¼ cup pomegranate seeds

1 Grease and lightly flour an 8×1½-inch round baking pan. Line the bottom of the pan with waxed paper. Grease and flour the waxed paper; set aside.

2 In a large bowl stir together flour, baking powder, and orange peel; set aside.

3 Place eggs and sugar in a blender container or food processor bowl. Cover and blend or process until smooth. Add almonds; blend or process about 1 minute or until nearly smooth. Stir the egg and almond mixture into the flour mixture. Spread batter evenly in prepared pan.

4 Bake in a 350° oven about 20 minutes or until lightly browned. Cool cake in pan on wire rack for 10 minutes. Remove cake from pan. Cool thoroughly on wire rack.

5 Meanwhile, combine orange juice and orange liqueur. Soak dried fruit in the orange mixture for 30 minutes. Drain, reserving orange mixture.

6 To serve, cut cake into 16 wedges. Arrange pear quarters, grapes and/or orange or grapefruit sections, pomegranate seeds, and dried fruit in 8 dessert bowls. Place 2 cake wedges in each bowl. Drizzle fruit and cake with reserved orange mixture.

Nutrition Facts per serving: 264 cal., 12 g total fat (1 g sat. fat), 53 mg chol., 43 mg sodium, 31 g carbo., 5 g fiber, 7 g pro. **Daily Values:** 26% vit. C, 10% calcium, 7% iron

MENU

Asian
Chicken Noodle Soup

Szechuan Shrimp

Egg Rolls

Vanilla Pear
Ice Cream

ASIAN CHICKEN NOODLE SOUP

Whether the recipe is written in Chinese or English, Spanish or Polish; whether it's flavored with carrots and celery or parsnips and potatoes, chicken soup is good for the body and soul. This one, with soy sauce, fresh ginger, and pea pods, demonstrates how a grandmother in Chinatown might make it.

Start to Finish: 20 minutes   **Makes:** 3 servings (5½ cups)

2 **14-ounce cans chicken broth**

1 **cup water**

¾ **cup dried fine egg noodles**

1 **tablespoon soy sauce**

1 **teaspoon grated fresh ginger**

⅛ **teaspoon crushed red pepper**

1 **medium red sweet pepper, cut into ¾-inch pieces**

1 **medium carrot, chopped**

⅓ **cup thinly sliced green onions**

1 **cup chopped cooked chicken or turkey**

1 **cup fresh pea pods, halved crosswise, or ½ of a 6-ounce package frozen pea pods, thawed and halved crosswise**

1 In a large saucepan combine chicken broth, water, noodles, soy sauce, ginger, and crushed red pepper. Bring to boiling. Stir in the sweet pepper, carrot, and green onions. Return to boiling; reduce heat. Simmer, covered, for 4 to 6 minutes or until vegetables are crisp-tender and noodles are tender.

2 Stir in chicken and pea pods. Simmer, uncovered, for 1 to 2 minutes more or until pea pods are crisp-tender.

33

Nutrition Facts per serving: 199 cal., 6 g total fat (1 g sat. fat), 50 mg chol., 1,466 mg sodium, 16 g carbo., 3 g fiber, 19 g pro. **Daily Values:** 162% vit. A, 161% vit. C, 4% calcium, 9% iron

SZECHUAN SHRIMP

It is believed that Indian Buddhist missionaries brought the incendiary spice so loved in Szechuan province on their travels down the famous Silk Road to China. Since then, residents of Jersey City, San Francisco, and locations in between have taken a liking to it too.

Start to Finish: 30 minutes   **Makes:** 4 servings

1 pound fresh or frozen shrimp in shells
3 tablespoons water
2 tablespoons catsup
1 tablespoon reduced-sodium soy sauce
1 tablespoon rice wine, dry sherry, or water
2 teaspoons cornstarch
1 teaspoon honey
1 teaspoon grated fresh ginger or ¼ teaspoon ground ginger

½ teaspoon crushed red pepper
1 tablespoon peanut oil or cooking oil
½ cup sliced green onions
4 cloves garlic, minced
2 cups cooked rice noodles or hot cooked rice
2 small red chile peppers, such as Fresno or Thai, sliced (optional)*

1 Thaw shrimp, if frozen. Peel and devein shrimp; cut in half lengthwise. Rinse; pat dry with paper towels. Set aside.

2 For sauce, in a small bowl stir together the water, catsup, soy sauce, rice wine, cornstarch, honey, ground ginger (if using), and crushed red pepper. Set aside.

3 Pour oil into a large skillet or wok. Heat over medium-high heat. Add green onions, garlic, and grated fresh ginger (if using); stir-fry for 30 seconds.

4 Add shrimp. Stir-fry for 2 to 3 minutes or until shrimp are opaque; push to side of skillet or wok. Stir sauce; add to center of skillet or wok. Cook and stir until thickened and bubbly. Cook and stir for 2 minutes more. Serve with rice noodles. If desired, garnish with sliced red chile peppers.

Nutrition Facts per serving: 257 cal., 5 g total fat (1 g sat. fat), 129 mg chol., 362 mg sodium, 30 g carbo., 0 g fiber, 20 g pro. **Daily Values:** 6% vit. A, 10% vit. C, 7% calcium, 18% iron

*Note: Because hot peppers, such as habañeros and other chiles, contain volatile oils that can burn your skin and eyes, avoid direct contact with them as much as possible. When working with chile peppers, wear plastic or rubber gloves. If your bare hands do touch the peppers, wash your hands well with soap and water.

EGG ROLLS

Every bite of these pork-filled egg rolls presents a symphony of tastes and textures: ginger, garlic, cabbage, and crunchy water chestnuts. Served with sweet-and-sour sauce (or maybe some head-clearing Chinese mustard), they're sure to make it to your list of classic favorites.

Prep: 25 minutes   **Cook:** 2 minutes per batch   **Oven:** 300°F   **Makes:** 8 egg rolls

8   egg roll skins
1   recipe Pork Filling
    Shortening or cooking oil for deep-fat frying

1⅓ cups bottled sweet-and-sour sauce or ½ cup prepared Chinese-style hot mustard

1 For each egg roll, place an egg roll skin on a flat surface with a corner toward you. Spoon about ¼ cup Pork Filling across and just below center of egg roll skin. Fold bottom corner over filling, tucking it under the filling. Fold sides over filling, forming an envelope shape. Roll egg roll toward remaining corner. Moisten top corner with water; press firmly to seal.

2 In a heavy saucepan or deep-fat fryer heat 2 inches of melted shortening to 365°F. Fry egg rolls, a few at a time, for 2 to 3 minutes or until golden brown. Drain on paper towels. Keep warm in a 300° oven while frying remaining egg rolls. Serve egg rolls warm with sweet-and-sour sauce.

Pork Filling: In a medium skillet cook 8 ounces ground pork, 1 teaspoon grated fresh ginger, and 1 clove garlic, minced, for 2 to 3 minutes or until meat is brown; drain off fat. Add ½ cup finely chopped bok choy or cabbage, ½ cup chopped water chestnuts, ½ cup shredded carrots, and ¼ cup finely chopped onion. Cook and stir for 2 minutes more. Combine 2 tablespoons soy sauce, 2 teaspoons cornstarch, ½ teaspoon sugar, and ¼ teaspoon salt; add to skillet. Cook and stir for 1 minute. Cool filling slightly.

Nutrition Facts per egg roll: 240 cal., 3 g total fat (1 g sat. fat), 16 mg chol., 794 mg sodium, 44 g carbo., 1 g fiber, 9 g pro. **Daily Values:** 46% vit. A, 17% vit. C, 8% calcium, 10% iron

VANILLA PEAR ICE CREAM

This beautiful ice cream, flecked with vanilla bean and fruit, is the perfect way to finish any Asian meal. Serve it with hot jasmine tea.

Prep: 10 minutes   **Cook:** 6 minutes   **Stand:** 30 minutes   **Chill:** 2 hours
Makes: 1 quart (8 servings)

1 **pound ripe fresh pears**	1 **cup whipping cream**
¼ **cup water**	⅔ **cup sugar**
1 **vanilla bean, split lengthwise**	½ **cup chopped almonds, toasted**
1 **cup half-and-half or light cream**	

1 Peel, core, and thinly slice pears. In a large skillet bring pears, water, and vanilla bean to boiling; reduce heat. Simmer, covered, about 6 minutes or until pears are tender. Remove from heat; do not drain. Let stand for 30 minutes. Remove vanilla bean; scrape any remaining seeds into pear mixture. Discard bean.

2 Place pear mixture in a food processor bowl or blender container. Cover and process or blend until smooth. Transfer pureed pear mixture to a medium bowl. Cover and chill at least 2 hours or overnight.

3 Stir half-and-half, whipping cream, and sugar into pear mixture. Freeze the mixture in a 2-, 3-, or 4-quart ice cream freezer according to manufacturer's directions. If desired, ripen up to 4 hours.

4 To serve, scoop ice cream into dessert dishes. Sprinkle with toasted almonds.

Nutrition Facts per ½-cup serving: 288 cal., 19 g total fat (9 g sat. fat), 52 mg chol., 24 mg sodium, 28 g carbo., 2 g fiber, 3 g pro. **Daily Values:** 12% vit. A, 3% vit. C, 8% calcium, 3% iron

37

MENU

* HOT + SOUR SOUP
* CABBAGE + PORK BAKED BUNS
* CASHEW PORK + BROCCOLI
* MU SHU PORK
* SESAME COOKIES*

*Purchase sesame cookies at Asian markets, specialty stores, or through mail order. See Resources, page 279.

HOT-AND-SOUR SOUP

To ensure the beaten egg forms delicate threads rather than wide ribbons, use a whisk to stir the egg into the hot soup.

Start to Finish: 30 minutes   **Makes:** 4 servings ($6\frac{2}{3}$ cups)

3½ **cups chicken broth**

2 **cups sliced fresh mushrooms**

3 **tablespoons rice vinegar or white vinegar**

2 **tablespoons soy sauce or reduced-sodium soy sauce**

1 **teaspoon sugar**

1 **teaspoon grated fresh ginger**

¼ **to ½ teaspoon black pepper**

1 **tablespoon cornstarch**

1 **tablespoon cold water**

2 **cups shredded cooked turkey**

2 **cups sliced bok choy**

1 **6-ounce package frozen pea pods**

1 **beaten egg**

3 **tablespoons thinly sliced green onions**

1 In a large saucepan combine chicken broth, mushrooms, vinegar, soy sauce, sugar, ginger, and pepper. Bring to boiling.

2 Meanwhile, stir together cornstarch and cold water; stir into broth mixture. Cook and stir until thickened and bubbly. Cook and stir for 2 minutes more. Stir in turkey, bok choy, and pea pods.

3 Pour the egg into the soup in a steady stream while stirring to create threads. Remove from heat. Stir in green onions.

Nutrition Facts per serving: 230 cal., 7 g total fat (2 g sat. fat), 106 mg chol., 1,431 mg sodium, 9 g carbo., 1 g fiber, 28 g pro. **Daily Values:** 25% vit. A, 32% vit. C, 9% calcium, 14% iron

Rice Vinegar: Made from rice wine, or sake, rice vinegar has a subtle tang and slightly sweet taste. Chinese rice vinegars are stronger than Japanese vinegars, although both are slightly milder than most vinegars. Chinese rice vinegar may be white (clear or pale yellow), used mainly in hot-and-sour or sweet-and-sour dishes; red, a typical accompaniment for boiled or steamed shellfish; or black, used mainly as a condiment.

39

CABBAGE- AND PORK- FILLED BAKED BUNS

Baking these pork-filled buns rather than steaming them the traditional way ensures even cooking throughout.

Prep: 1 hour   **Rise:** 1 hour   **Bake:** 15 minutes   **Oven:** 350°F   **Makes:** 15 appetizer buns

3 to 3½ cups all-purpose flour	½ teaspoon salt
1 package active dry yeast	2 eggs
1 cup milk	1 recipe Pork and Cabbage Filling
¼ cup sugar	1 tablespoon water
2 tablespoons butter or margarine	Black and white sesame seeds (optional)

1 In a large mixing bowl stir together 1½ cups of the flour and the yeast. In a small saucepan heat milk, sugar, butter, and salt just until warm (120°F to 130°F). Add to flour mixture. Add 1 of the eggs. Beat with an electric mixer on low speed for 30 seconds, scraping sides of bowl constantly. Beat on high speed for 3 minutes. Using a wooden spoon, stir in as much of the remaining flour as you can.

2 On a lightly floured surface knead in enough of the remaining flour to make a moderately soft dough that is smooth and elastic (knead 3 to 5 minutes total). Shape into a ball. Place in a lightly greased bowl, turning once to grease the surface. Cover and let rise in a warm place until doubled (about 1 hour). Meanwhile, prepare Pork and Cabbage Filling. Set filling aside to cool.

3 Punch dough down. Turn dough out onto a lightly floured surface. Shape dough into 15 balls. Cover and let rest for 10 minutes.

4 Line an extra-large baking sheet with foil; grease foil. Roll or pat each ball of dough into a 4-inch circle. Brush edges with water. Place about 2 tablespoons filling into center of each dough circle. Bring up edges of dough around filling, stretching dough just until edges meet; pinch to seal. Place buns, seam side down, on prepared baking sheet. In a small bowl combine the remaining egg and the water. Brush egg mixture evenly over buns. If desired, sprinkle with sesame seeds. Bake in a 350° oven for 15 to 18 minutes or until buns are golden. Transfer buns to a wire rack to cool slightly. Serve warm.

Pork and Cabbage Filling: In a small bowl stir together 2 tablespoons soy sauce, 1 teaspoon cornstarch, 1 teaspoon sugar, ½ teaspoon toasted sesame oil, and ¼ teaspoon ground black pepper; set aside. In a large skillet cook and stir 1 teaspoon grated fresh ginger and 1 clove garlic, minced, in 1 tablespoon hot butter for 15 seconds. Add 3 cups finely shredded baby bok choy or Chinese cabbage, 1 cup chopped fresh shiitake mushrooms, ¾ cup shredded carrots, and ½ cup thinly sliced green onions. Cook and stir for 2 minutes. Remove from skillet. Add 1 tablespoon butter to skillet. Add 8 ounces chopped lean pork to skillet. Cook and stir about 2 minutes or until pork is no longer pink. Return vegetable mixture to skillet. Add soy sauce mixture. Cook and stir for 2 minutes. Remove from heat; set aside to cool.

Nutrition Facts per appetizer: 179 cal., 5 g total fat (2 g sat. fat), 46 mg chol., 268 mg sodium, 23 g carbo., 1 g fiber, 8 g pro.
Daily Values: 47% vit. A, 13% vit. C, 5% calcium, 9% iron

A rested dough is easy to roll.

Pinch together over filling to seal.

CASHEW PORK AND BROCCOLI

Originally from India, sweet and buttery cashew nuts made their way to Central and South America via Portuguese explorers during the time of Christopher Columbus. They eventually reached China where they became an important ingredient in stir-fries such as this one.

Prep: 35 minutes   **Marinate:** 1 hour   **Cook:** 10 minutes   **Makes:** 4 servings

12 ounces lean boneless pork	1 teaspoon sugar
2 tablespoons soy sauce	⅛ teaspoon crushed red pepper
2 teaspoons toasted sesame oil	1 tablespoon cooking oil
2 teaspoons grated fresh ginger	2 medium onions, cut into thin wedges
2 cloves garlic, minced	2 stalks celery, thinly bias-sliced (1 cup)
½ cup hoisin sauce	3 cups broccoli florets
½ cup water	2 cups hot cooked rice
2 tablespoons soy sauce	½ cup dry roasted cashews
1 tablespoon cornstarch	

1 Trim fat from pork. Partially freeze pork. Thinly slice across grain into bite-size strips. In a medium bowl stir together pork, 2 tablespoons soy sauce, sesame oil, ginger, and garlic. Cover and refrigerate for 1 to 2 hours.

2 For sauce, in a small bowl stir together hoisin sauce, water, 2 tablespoons soy sauce, cornstarch, sugar, and crushed red pepper; set aside.

3 Pour the cooking oil into a wok or large skillet. (Add more oil as necessary during cooking.) Preheat over medium-high heat. Stir-fry onions and celery in hot oil for 1 minute. Add the broccoli; stir-fry for 3 to 4 minutes or until the vegetables are crisp-tender. Remove vegetables from the wok.

4 Add pork mixture to the hot wok. Stir-fry for 2 to 3 minutes or until cooked through. Push pork from center of wok.

5 Stir sauce; pour sauce into center of wok. Cook and stir until sauce is thickened and bubbly. Return cooked vegetables to wok. Stir all ingredients together to coat with sauce. Cook, covered, for 1 minute more or until heated through. Serve immediately with hot cooked rice. Sprinkle with roasted cashews.

Make-ahead tip: Prepare vegetables; cover and chill for up to 4 hours.

Nutrition Facts per serving: 493 cal., 20 g total fat (4 g sat. fat), 50 mg chol., 1,350 mg sodium, 49 g carbo., 4 g fiber, 29 g pro. **Daily Values:** 24% vit. A, 95% vit. C, 9% calcium, 19% iron

MU SHU PORK

In the melting pot of America, it's OK to mix and match ethnic cuisines when the necessity of convenience calls for culinary invention. Although Mu Shu Pork traditionally is served tucked into delicate and time-consuming Mandarin pancakes, this quicker-to-make version calls for flour tortillas.

Prep: 25 minutes   **Bake:** 10 minutes   **Stand:** 10 minutes   **Oven:** 350°F   **Makes:** 4 servings

8   8-inch fat-free flour tortillas
¼   cup reduced-sodium soy sauce
2   teaspoons cornstarch
8   ounces pork tenderloin, cut into bite-size strips
2   teaspoons cooking or peanut oil
1   teaspoon hot chile oil or ¼ teaspoon crushed red pepper

2   cloves garlic, minced
2   cups shredded coleslaw mix (with cabbage and carrots)
2   cups fresh bean sprouts
½   cup sliced green onions
½   cup prepared plum sauce

1 Wrap tortillas tightly in foil. Heat in a 350° oven for 10 to 15 minutes to soften.*

2 In a bowl combine soy sauce and cornstarch. Add pork and toss to coat; let stand 10 minutes.

3 Heat cooking oil and chile oil in a large nonstick skillet over medium-high heat. Add pork mixture and garlic; stir-fry for 2 minutes. Add 1 cup of the coleslaw mix, the bean sprouts, and green onions; continue to stir-fry for 3 to 4 minutes or until pork is cooked through and vegetables are crisp-tender.

4 Sprinkle the remaining 1 cup coleslaw mix over center of tortillas. Divide pork mixture among tortillas; fold tortillas in half over filling and fold in half again, forming a triangle. Serve with plum sauce.

*Note: To soften tortillas in a microwave oven, place four tortillas between microwave-safe paper towels. Cook on 100% power (high) for 45 to 60 seconds or until softened. Repeat with remaining four tortillas. Keep tortillas covered until ready to use.

Nutrition Facts per serving: 449 cal., 5 g total fat (1 g sat. fat), 36 mg chol., 1,451 mg sodium, 77 g carbo., 4 g fiber, 20 g pro. **Daily Values:** 4% vit. A, 42% vit. C, 6% calcium, 27% iron

MENU

Mushroom, Noodle, and Tofu Soup

Green Curry Chicken

Chicken Pad Thai

Ginger Custard

MUSHROOM, NOODLE, AND TOFU SOUP

Similar to spaghetti but of Japanese origin, udon noodles are made with either wheat or corn flour. You can find them fresh or dried in Asian markets or in the Asian section of your supermarket.

Start to Finish: 30 minutes   **Makes:** 6 servings (9 cups)

1   49-ounce can reduced-sodium chicken broth (about 6 cups)

1   10- to 12-ounce package extra-firm tofu (fresh bean curd), drained and cut into ½-inch cubes

1   tablespoon soy sauce

1   tablespoon toasted sesame oil

6   ounces sliced fresh shiitake or button mushrooms (about 2¼ cups)

1   tablespoon grated fresh ginger

1   clove garlic, minced

1   tablespoon cooking oil

1   16-ounce package frozen sugar snap stir-fry vegetables

2   ounces dried udon noodles or spaghetti, broken

1   tablespoon snipped fresh cilantro

1 In a large saucepan bring the broth to boiling. Meanwhile, in a medium bowl gently stir together tofu cubes, soy sauce, and sesame oil; set aside.

2 In a medium saucepan cook the sliced mushrooms, ginger, and garlic in hot cooking oil for 4 minutes. Add to the hot broth. Stir in the frozen vegetables and udon noodles. Bring to boiling; reduce heat.

3 Simmer, covered, for 10 to 12 minutes or until vegetables and noodles are tender, stirring once or twice. Gently stir in the tofu mixture and the cilantro; heat through.

Nutrition Facts per serving: 169 cal., 8 g total fat (1 g sat. fat), 0 mg chol., 791 mg sodium, 14 g carbo., 2 g fiber, 10 g pro. **Daily Values:** 29% vit. A, 21% vit. C, 5% calcium, 8% iron

GREEN CURRY CHICKEN

Servers at Thai restaurants have been known to ask customers how they want their curry, based on a scale of stars. One star represents a little bit of lip tingling; at the other end of the scale, four stars designates a four-alarm experience. Add the green curry paste according to your own heat meter.

Prep: 20 minutes   **Cook:** 30 minutes   **Makes:** 4 servings

- 4 skinless, boneless chicken breast halves (about 1½ pounds total)
- 2 tablespoons cooking oil
- 1 to 2 tablespoons green curry paste
- 1 13½-ounce can unsweetened coconut milk
- 8 ounces fresh small green beans, trimmed (2 cups)
- 2 tablespoons fish sauce
- ¼ cup torn fresh basil leaves
- 2 cups hot cooked rice

1 Cut chicken into bite-size strips. In a large nonstick wok or skillet cook and stir half of the chicken in 1 tablespoon of the hot oil over medium-high heat for 3 to 4 minutes or until no longer pink. Remove chicken from wok. Cook remaining chicken; remove from wok.

2 Add curry paste and the remaining 1 tablespoon oil to wok. Cook and stir for 2 minutes. Carefully add coconut milk, stirring to blend. Simmer, uncovered, for 10 minutes.

47

3 Add green beans and fish sauce to coconut milk mixture in wok. Simmer, uncovered, for 5 minutes. Add chicken; simmer for 3 minutes more. Remove from heat. Stir in basil. Serve with hot cooked rice.

Nutrition Facts per serving: 573 cal., 29 g total fat (17 g sat. fat), 98 mg chol., 710 mg sodium, 31 g carbo., 2 g fiber, 44 g pro. **Daily Values:** 9% vit. A, 15% vit. C, 8% calcium, 23% iron

CHICKEN PAD THAI

Whether they're called *bahn pho* (in Vietnamese) or *sen-mee* (in Thai), rice stick noodles are still rice stick noodles. The foundation for this famous dish, they also give Chinese lo mein some hearty competition when it comes to popularity. Don't oversoak the rice noodles or they'll break when cooked.

Prep: 15 minutes   **Cook:** 15 minutes   **Makes:** 4 servings

½ pound dried rice noodles (Vietnamese bahn pho or Thai sen-mee)

¼ cup salted peanuts, finely chopped

1 tablespoon granulated sugar

½ teaspoon grated lime peel

2 tablespoons fish sauce

2 tablespoons fresh lime juice

1½ teaspoons dried shrimp paste or mashed anchovy

1 tablespoon Asian chile sauce

2 tablespoons packed brown sugar

4½ teaspoons rice vinegar

3 tablespoons vegetable oil

¼ cup chopped shallots

1 pound boneless, skinless chicken breasts, cut into 3-inch strips

1 tablespoon finely chopped garlic

1 large egg, lightly beaten

1 cup fresh bean sprouts

⅓ cup sliced green onions

2 tablespoons chopped fresh cilantro

1 Place noodles in a large bowl. Add enough hot tap water to cover; let stand 10 to 15 minutes until pliable but not soft. Drain well in a colander.

2 Meanwhile, for peanut topping, in a cup combine peanuts, granulated sugar, and lime peel; set aside.

3 In a small bowl combine fish sauce, lime juice, shrimp paste, chile sauce, brown sugar, and rice vinegar; stir until smooth. Set aside.

4 Heat 1 tablespoon of the oil in a 12-inch nonstick skillet over medium-high heat. Add shallots and cook 2 minutes or until softened and light brown. Add chicken and garlic; cook and stir for 6 minutes or until chicken browns. Transfer to a bowl.

5 Add egg to the hot skillet and cook for 30 seconds. Turn egg with spatula and cook 30 to 60 seconds more or just until set. Remove and chop; set aside.

6 Heat the remaining 2 tablespoons oil in skillet over high heat for 30 seconds. Add drained noodles and sprouts; stir-fry for 2 minutes. Add fish sauce mixture and chicken; cook 1 to 2 minutes more or until heated through. Divide chicken mixture among 4 serving plates. Sprinkle servings with egg and peanut topping. Garnish with green onions and cilantro.

Nutrition Facts per serving: 565 cal., 19 g total fat (3 g sat. fat), 120 mg chol., 838 mg sodium, 68 g carbo., 1 g fiber, 33 g pro. **Daily Values:** 5% calcium,

GINGER CUSTARD

Pick your ginger. The crystallized (or candied) version gives this aromatic custard a fiery flavor and chewy texture. Ground ginger is milder and produces a custard that's as smooth as silk.

Prep: 15 minutes   **Bake:** 35 minutes   **Chill:** several hours   **Oven:** 325°F   **Makes:** 4 servings

4 **egg yolks**	1 **tablespoon finely chopped crystallized**
⅓ **cup sugar**	**ginger or ½ teaspoon ground ginger**
1½ **cups whole milk**	

1 In a medium bowl whisk together the egg yolks and sugar until well combined. Gradually stir in the milk. Stir in ground ginger, if using.

2 Place four 6-ounce custard cups in a 2-quart square baking dish. Divide egg mixture among custard cups. Sprinkle crystallized ginger, if using, over tops of custard cups. Place dish on oven rack. Pour boiling water into the baking dish around custard cups to a depth of 1 inch.

3 Bake in a 325° oven for 35 to 45 minutes or until edges of custard are firm and center appears nearly set when lightly shaken. Cool slightly. Chill several hours before serving.

Nutrition Facts per serving: 180 cal., 8 g total fat (3 g sat. fat), 225 mg chol., 52 mg sodium, 21 g carbo., 0 g fiber, 25 g pro. **Daily Values: 9**% vit. A, 1% vit. C, 13% calcium, 4% iron

TODAY

TERIYAKI BEEF &
LETTUCE WRAPS

WONTON SOUP

VEGETABLE FRIED RICE

MMM.. BANANA
WONTONS.

TERIYAKI BEEF AND LETTUCE WRAPS

Long before wraps became the rage in America, Asian cooks folded savory fillings in rice-paper wrappers, very thin pancakes, and lettuce leaves.

Prep: 15 minutes   **Cook:** 10 minutes   **Makes:** 4 servings

1 head iceberg lettuce

2 large carrots, shredded

1 large green sweet pepper, cut into thin strips

4 tablespoons rice wine vinegar

¼ teaspoon salt

1 pound lean ground beef

4 tablespoons roasted-garlic teriyaki marinade and sauce

1 to 2 red Thai chile peppers or 1 jalapeño chile pepper, seeded and minced*

1 tablespoon water

1 Core lettuce. Carefully remove at least 8 whole leaves; set aside. Slice enough of the remaining lettuce to equal 1 cup. In a bowl toss the sliced lettuce, carrots, sweet pepper, 3 tablespoons of the rice wine vinegar, and the salt.

2 In a medium bowl toss the beef with 3 tablespoons of the roasted-garlic teriyaki sauce. Heat a large nonstick skillet over medium-high heat. Shape beef into ½-inch pieces. Add half of the pieces to the hot skillet. Cook for 3 minutes, turning, until brown on all sides; transfer to a bowl. Repeat with remaining beef.

3 Return all the beef to the skillet; add chile peppers, water, and the remaining 1 tablespoon of vinegar and 1 tablespoon of teriyaki sauce; bring to simmering. Cook, covered, for 3 minutes.

4 Spoon beef and vegetable mixture into lettuce leaves; roll up.

Nutrition Facts per serving: 250 cal., 11 g total fat (4 g sat. fat), 71 mg chol., 936 mg sodium, 13 g carbo., 2 g fiber, 22 g pro. **Daily Values:** 236% vit. A, 69% vit. C, 4% calcium, 16% iron

*See note, page 35.

51

WONTON SOUP

Wrapping wontons may be time-consuming, but the fresh chicken filling makes every seam worth the effort. This recipe makes enough wontons for two batches of soup. Freeze the half you don't use for an easy meal next time.

Prep: 45 minutes   **Cook:** 15 minutes   **Chill:** 15 minutes   **Makes:** 6 servings

1 pound ground raw chicken
⅓ cup finely chopped canned water chestnuts
2 tablespoons chopped green onion
1 tablespoon soy sauce
2 teaspoons grated fresh ginger
1 teaspoon rice vinegar
1 teaspoon finely chopped garlic

1 teaspoon toasted sesame oil
½ teaspoon sugar
1 14-ounce package wonton wrappers (about 60)
4 14-ounce cans chicken broth
½ teaspoon soy sauce
1 cup fresh baby spinach or chopped fresh spinach

1 For wonton filling, in a medium bowl combine chicken, water chestnuts, green onions, the 1 tablespoon soy sauce, ginger, vinegar, garlic, sesame oil, and sugar. Cover and chill for 15 minutes.

2 Meanwhile, line two 15×10×1-inch baking pans with waxed paper; set aside. In the center of 1 wonton wrapper place 1½ teaspoons chicken mixture. Brush the edge of wrapper with water. Fold sides of wrapper together to form a triangle; lightly pinch edge and seal. Bring long ends over center, overlapping slightly. Transfer to prepared pan and cover loosely with a sheet of waxed paper. Repeat for remaining filling and wrappers, dividing the wontons between the two pans. Cover with plastic wrap and refrigerate 1 pan of wontons. (Freeze remaining wontons for 1 hour or until firm. Transfer to a large resealable freezer storage bag and freeze for up to 2 weeks.*)

3 Bring a large Dutch oven of salted water to boiling. In another large Dutch oven bring broth and the ½ teaspoon soy sauce to boiling; reduce heat and simmer, uncovered, for 10 minutes. When salted water comes to a boil, add one-third of the refrigerated wontons. Cook until wontons begin to float to the surface, about 1 to 2 minutes; carefully stir wontons to prevent sticking. Use a slotted spoon to transfer wontons to simmering broth. Repeat with remaining refrigerated wontons; add spinach and heat through.

*Note: To cook frozen wontons, prepare recipe for soup as directed, except cook the frozen wontons (do not defrost) in boiling water for 2 to 4 minutes.

Nutrition Facts per serving: 347 cal., 10 g total fat (1 g sat. fat), 8 mg chol., 1,525 mg sodium, 43 g carbo., 1 g fiber, 21 g pro. **Daily Values:** 6% vit. A, 3% vit. C, 4% calcium, 12% iron

VEGETABLE FRIED RICE

For a perfectly fluffy platter of steaming fried rice, chill the cooked rice thoroughly before stir-frying with the vegetables and flavorings.

Prep: 30 minutes   **Cook:** 7 minutes   **Makes:** about 3 cups (4 side-dish servings)

- 1 teaspoon toasted sesame oil or cooking oil
- 1 beaten egg
- 1 cup fresh asparagus cut into 1-inch pieces
- ¼ cup chopped fresh mushrooms
- ¼ cup bias-sliced celery (½ stalk)
- 2 tablespoons thinly sliced green onion

- 2 cloves garlic, minced
- 1 tablespoon cooking oil
- 3 tablespoons reduced-sodium soy sauce
- 2 tablespoons dry white wine or water
  Dash ground red pepper
- 2 cups chilled cooked rice

1 In a large skillet heat the 1 teaspoon sesame oil over medium heat. Add egg, lifting and tilting the skillet to form a thin layer of egg (egg may not completely cover the bottom of the skillet). Cook for 1 minute or until egg is set. Invert skillet over a baking sheet to remove cooked egg; cut into short, narrow strips (about 3×½ inch). Set egg strips aside.

2 In the same skillet cook and stir asparagus, mushrooms, celery, green onion, and garlic in the 1 tablespoon cooking oil about 4 minutes or until the asparagus and celery are crisp-tender. Stir in soy sauce, wine, and ground red pepper. Add cooked rice. Cook and stir about 2 minutes or until mixture is heated through. Stir in egg strips. Serve immediately.

Nutrition Facts per side-dish serving: 188 cal., 6 g total fat (1 g sat. fat), 53 mg chol., 458 mg sodium, 25 g carbo., 1 g fiber, 6 g pro. **Daily Values:** 4% vit. A, 16% vit. C, 3% calcium, 9% iron

BANANA WONTONS

Not your ordinary wontons, these sweet banana-filled bundles pair up with Orange Caramel Sauce instead of broth.

Prep: 30 minutes   **Cook:** 1 to 2 minutes per batch   **Oven:** 300°F   **Makes:** 4 to 6 servings

Cooking oil or shortening for deep-fat frying

2 medium ripe bananas, peeled and finely chopped (1 cup)

2 tablespoons packed brown sugar

1 teaspoon finely shredded orange peel

½ teaspoon ground cinnamon

18 wonton wrappers

1 recipe Orange Caramel Sauce

1 teaspoon sesame seeds, toasted

1 In a wok or large saucepan heat 1½ to 2 inches cooking oil to 365°F. Meanwhile, for filling, in a small bowl stir together bananas, brown sugar, orange peel, and cinnamon.

2 For each wonton, place a wonton wrapper with a point toward you. Spoon a slightly rounded teaspoon of banana mixture just below center. Fold bottom point over filling; tuck point under filling. Roll wonton wrapper once or twice to cover the filling, leaving about 1 inch unrolled at top of wrapper. Moisten the right-hand corner of wrapper with a little water. Grasp the right- and left-hand corners of wrapper. Bring these corners toward you. Overlap the left-hand and right-hand corners. Press corners together securely to seal.

3 Fry a few wontons at a time in hot oil for 1 to 2 minutes or until golden, turning once. Remove from oil. Drain on paper towels. Keep warm in a 300° oven while frying remaining wontons.

4 To serve, arrange wontons on dessert plates. Drizzle with Orange Caramel Sauce and sprinkle with sesame seeds.

Orange Caramel Sauce: In a small saucepan stir together ½ cup packed brown sugar and 1 teaspoon cornstarch. Stir in ½ cup whipping cream, 1 tablespoon butter, and 2 teaspoons Grand Marnier or orange juice. Cook and stir over medium heat until thickened and bubbly. Cook and stir for 2 minutes more. Serve warm over wontons. Makes about 1 cup.

Nutrition Facts per serving: 503 cal., 22 g total fat (10 g sat. fat), 52 mg chol., 263 mg sodium, 73 g carbo., 2 g fiber, 5 g pro. **Daily Values:** 12% vit. A, 11% vit. C, 8% calcium, 13% iron

TIRAMISU

MACARONI·MA
RAVIOLI·MAKI
SPAGHETTI B
ITALIAN & ENGLIS

PIZZA
FOCACCIA
PIZZA
Ricotta
PROSCIUTTO BA

Salads

Fennel and Orange Salad, 93
Fresh Mozzarella Salad, 87
Italian Salad with Garlic Polenta Croutons, 74
Marinated Antipasto, 98

Soups

Italian Country Bread Soup, 81
Lemon, Egg, and Parmesan Soup, 63
Minestrone, 105
White Bean, Garlic, and Sage Soup, 68

Italian

Entrées

Arugula, Tomato, and Olive Sauce, 66
Chicken Stuffed with Smoked Mozzarella, 100
Creamy Tomato Sauce, 75
Eggplant and Dried Tomato Pasta, 106
Gnocchi, 76
Homemade Fettucine, 64
Italian Sausages with Polenta, 89
Orzo with Chicken and Mushrooms, 70
Pork and Porcini Bolognese, 82
Risotto with Leeks and Roasted Asparagus, 95

Side Dishes

Caponatina, 88
Focaccia, 78
Homemade Pesto with Linguine, 102
Oven-Baked Broccoli, 83
Roasted Asparagus and Red Peppers, 71
Zucchini alla Romana, 99

Desserts

Biscotti, 103
Cannoli, 90
Honey-Baked Pears, 96
Lemon Ice Cream, 72
Nonna's Chocolate Cookies, 79
Polenta and Plum Cake, 85
Walnut-Cappucino Torte, 107

Proud Italian-Americans love to point out that America was "discovered" by an Italian (Christopher Columbus, born Cristoforo Colombo in Genoa, Italy) and that both North and South America were named after another (Amerigo Vespucci of Florence).

Some of the most popular foods in the United States today, from dozens of pastas and sauces to pizza and ice cream, come straight from Italy. Italian food wouldn't be so popular if it wasn't so good; it even prompted playwright Neil Simon to quip, "There are two laws in the universe: The Law of Gravity and Everybody Likes Italian Food."

Americans' love affair with Italian food grew, in part, thanks to the millions of Italian immigrants who began arriving in the late 19th century. With them they brought their culture and their luscious cuisine. The large wave of immigration that would eventually lead more than 5 million Italians across the Atlantic Ocean began sometime during the late 1870s to early 1880s. The majority of immigrants came from southern Italy, the birthplace of Neapolitan pizza, unique pastas and sauces, and the sweet frozen dessert treat called gelato.

By the 1920s, more Italians lived in New York City than in Florence, but it wasn't until the word pasta replaced the more universal macaroni in the 1960s that Americans began to wake up to the fact that Italian food encompassed pasta and pizza and great-tasting dishes such as polenta and risotto too.

Italian immigrants are known for clinging tenaciously to culinary roots that remind them of home. This persistence prompted 20th-century social workers, who attempted to assimilate immigrants, to report that the gastronomically stubborn Italians were "not yet Americanized, still eating Italian food." Not only are their descendants still eating it, all of America has joined them at the table.

plum, or roma tomato

arborio rice

eggplant

Parmigiano-Reggiano, or Parmesan cheese

olive oil

oregano

Most Americans become familiar with Italian ingredients because so much Italian cuisine has been absorbed into everyday American cooking. Yet, in fact, we may have reached the point where some key Italian ingredients are taken for granted—without thought given to their origin or historical significance. Let's consider just a few.

Tomatoes, for many, are the quintessential Italian ingredient, but they actually originated in Peru. From there they were brought to Spain and Italy but for many years were grown only as ornamental plants there because the fruit was thought to be poisonous. When many of us think of Italian tomatoes, we think of the plum tomato (also known as roma, or Italian plum tomato), which is marvelous in tomato-based pasta sauces. Excellent canned versions of these tomatoes, such as San Marzano, are also available, adding to the plum variety's popularity.

Many cuisines of the world feature some form of noodles or **pasta,** but perhaps no single cuisine has become as closely identified with pasta as that of Italy. Although it is a common myth that Marco Polo brought pasta back with him from Asia, there is evidence that noodles existed in Italy well before his return at the end of the 13th century. At any rate, the virtuosity with which Italians have made use of this culinary medium is amazing in its breadth and diversity.

Americans' wholesale adoption of pasta soared with the influx of Italian immigrants in the late 19th century, but this was by no means the earliest encounter Americans had with pasta. It may have been introduced quite early by the Spanish, and it was also enjoyed by Thomas Jefferson—a gourmand and American president.

Italian cheeses may have no rival in the world except perhaps those of its neighbor to the west, France. Among the many outstanding cheeses of Italy, the king of them all, and the one that many Americans have embraced above all, is Parmesan, or in its ultimate expression, **Parmigiano-Reggiano,** imported from the Italian provinces of Reggio-Emilia and Parma. The imported version of this cow's-milk cheese features an intense, buttery, sharp flavor that is delectable either by itself or incorporated into Italian dishes.

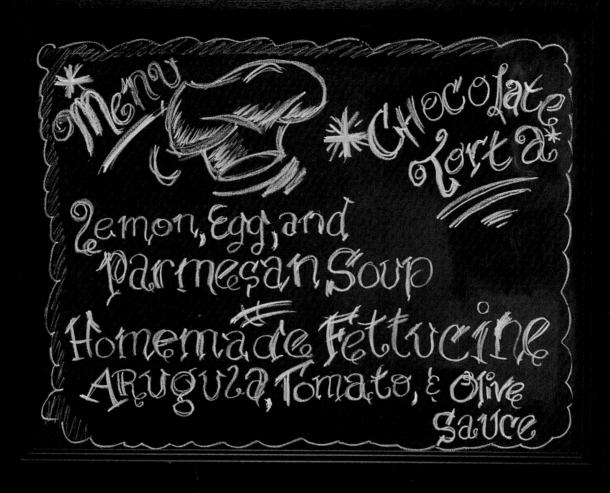

Menu

Chocolate Torta

Lemon, Egg, and Parmesan Soup

Homemade Fettucine Arugula, Tomato, & Olive Sauce

*Torta is a special type of Italian cake that can be purchased at an Italian bakery or market, or see Resources, page 279.

LEMON, EGG, AND PARMESAN SOUP

This soup makes a lovely and light starter to a multicourse Italian-style feast.

Start to Finish: 15 minutes   **Makes:** 8 servings

- **8 cups chicken stock or broth**
- **2 tablespoons finely shredded lemon peel (set aside)**
- **2 tablespoons lemon juice**
- **⅓ cup grated Parmesan cheese**
- **Salt and white pepper**
- **3 eggs, beaten**
- **2 tablespoons snipped fresh marjoram or oregano**

1 In a Dutch oven or large saucepan, heat chicken stock and lemon juice to simmering.

2 Stir in lemon peel and Parmesan. Season to taste with salt and white pepper.

3 Pour the beaten eggs into the soup in a steady steam while stirring two or three times to create shreds. Stir in marjoram; serve immediately.

Nutrition Facts per serving: 84 cal., 4 g total fat (1 g sat. fat), 82 mg chol., 861 mg sodium, 2 g carbo., 0 g fiber, 8 g pro.
Daily Values: 3% vit. A, 7% vit. C, 7% calcium, 5% iron

HOMEMADE FETTUCCINE

Even the highest quality, most expensive box of dried pasta doesn't come close to the taste and texture of fresh pasta. Making homemade pasta with an old-fashioned pasta machine is an especially fun thing to do with kids. Let them turn the crank, and the noodles (and the giggles) will soon come rolling out.

Prep: 1 hour   **Cook:** 2 minutes   **Makes:** 8 main-dish servings (about 1 pound pasta)

2⅓ **cups all-purpose flour**
½ **teaspoon salt**
2 **beaten eggs**

⅓ **cup water**
1 **teaspoon cooking oil or olive oil**

1 In a large bowl stir together 2 cups of the flour and the salt. Make a well in center of the flour mixture. In a small bowl combine eggs, water, and oil. Add egg mixture to flour mixture; stir to combine.

2 Sprinkle a clean kneading surface with the remaining ⅓ cup flour. Turn dough out onto floured surface. Knead until dough is smooth and elastic (8 to 10 minutes total). Cover and let the dough rest for 10 minutes.

3 Divide the dough into 4 equal portions. On a lightly floured surface, roll each dough portion into a long oval (about 1/16 inch thick). Sprinkle lightly with flour. Starting at short end, roll dough into a tube. Cut into ¼-inch strips. (If using a pasta machine, pass each portion through machine according to manufacturer's directions until dough is 1/16 inch thick. Let stand; cut as desired.) Unroll strips.

4 To serve pasta immediately, cook pasta in lightly boiling salted water for 2 minutes; drain.

5 To store cut pasta, hang it from a pasta-drying rack or clothes hanger, or spread it on a wire cooling rack. Let pasta dry overnight or until completely dry. Place in an airtight container and chill up to 3 days. Or dry the pasta at least 1 hour; place it in a freezer bag or freezer container and freeze for up to 8 months.

Food processor directions: Place steel blade in food processor bowl. Add flour, salt, and eggs to bowl. Cover and process until mixture forms fine crumbs about the consistency of cornmeal. With the processor running, slowly pour water and oil through the feed tube. Continue processing just until the dough forms a ball. Transfer dough to a lightly floured surface. Cover; let dough rest for 10 minutes. Continue as directed in Step 3.

Nutrition Facts per main-dish serving: 145 cal., 2 g total fat (1 g sat. fat), 53 mg chol., 162 mg sodium, 26 g carbo., 1 g fiber, 5 g pro. **Daily Values:** 2% vit. A, 1% calcium, 10% iron

64

Make a well in the flour before adding liquid.

Once the dough has been flattened, roll into a long tube.

With a sharp knife, slice down quickly to form individual noodles.

ARUGULA, TOMATO, AND OLIVE SAUCE

Peppery arugula, known as *rucola* in Italian, has gradually gained popularity in America. It's great for fresh salads and summery sauces like this one.

Start to Finish: 25 minutes   **Makes:** 4 servings

3   cloves garlic, minced

¼   teaspoon crushed red pepper

3   tablespoons olive oil

4   to 5 cups torn arugula

¼   teaspoon salt

2   medium roma tomatoes, chopped

1   cup pitted niçoise or kalamata olives, halved

3   tablespoons snipped fresh parsley

¼   cup grated Parmesan cheese

Hot cooked pasta (optional)

1 In a large skillet cook garlic and red pepper in hot olive oil for 3 to 4 minutes or until garlic is tender. Stir in arugula and salt. Cook and stir over medium heat just until arugula begins to wilt. Stir in tomatoes, olives, and parsley; heat through. If desired, toss with hot cooked pasta. Sprinkle with Parmesan cheese.

Nutrition Facts per serving (sauce only): 152 cal., 13 g total fat (2 g sat. fat), 4 mg chol., 622 mg sodium, 7 g carbo., 2 g fiber, 3 g pro. **Daily Values:** 15% vit. A, 23% vit. C, 10% calcium, 4% iron

66

The incredible olive: After 6,000 years of cultivation, olives are more popular than ever—and for good reason. They're so versatile you can stew them with meats and vegetables, stir them into risotto, toss them with salads or pasta, or whirl them with garlic and oil into a rich tapenade.

Most olives are cured in a saltwater brine, but some varieties are dry-cured in salt, oil-cured, wine-cured, or dry-roasted. Salt- and dry-cured olives are wrinkled, soft, and leathery. Brine-cured, oil-cured, and wine-cured olives are plump and moist. Olives range in size from small to colossal, depending on the variety. You can purchase green olives unpitted or pitted, and stuffed with pimientos, anchovies, whole almonds, or tiny onions. Black olives are available unpitted, pitted, sliced, and chopped.

MENU

White Bean, Garlic,
+ Sage Soup

•

Orzo with Chicken
+ mushrooms

•

Roasted Asparagus
+ Red Peppers

•

Lemon Ice Cream

WHITE BEAN, GARLIC, AND SAGE SOUP

Tuscans love legumes so much that outsiders once disparagingly dubbed them "bean-eaters." Since then, however, the love for legumes has gone global. Serve this sage-infused soup with slices of toasted bread brushed with olive oil and rubbed with garlic.

Prep: 25 minutes   **Stand:** 1 hour   **Cook:** 1 hour   **Makes:** 8 to 10 appetizer servings

1 pound dry Great Northern or navy beans

1 cup chopped onion

1 tablespoon olive oil

2 tablespoons bottled minced garlic or 12 cloves garlic, minced

4 14-ounce cans chicken broth

2 tablespoons snipped fresh sage

½ teaspoon coarse ground black pepper

Salt

1 Rinse beans. In a 4-quart Dutch oven combine beans and 8 cups water. Bring to boiling; reduce heat. Simmer for 2 minutes. Remove from heat. Cover and let stand for 1 hour. (Or place beans in water in a Dutch oven. Cover and let soak overnight.) Drain and rinse beans; set aside.

2 In the same Dutch oven cook onion in hot oil over medium heat until tender. Add garlic; cook and stir for 1 minute. Stir in beans and broth. Bring to boiling; reduce heat. Simmer, covered, for 1 to 1½ hours or until beans are tender. Stir in sage and pepper; season to taste with salt.

Nutrition Facts per appetizer serving: 254 cal., 3 g total fat (0 g sat. fat), 0 mg chol., 712 mg sodium, 39 g carbo., 12 g fiber, 17 g pro. **Daily Values:** 7% vit. C, 11% calcium, 16% iron

68

ORZO WITH CHICKEN AND MUSHROOMS

Don't settle for plain pasta. Cook the orzo in herb-seasoned chicken broth for a boost of extra flavor.

Prep: 20 minutes   **Cook:** 20 minutes   **Makes:** 4 servings

2¾ **cups chicken broth**

2¼ **cups water**

½ **teaspoon Italian seasoning, crushed**

½ **pound boneless, skinless chicken thighs, cut into ½-inch cubes**

¼ **teaspoon salt**

¼ **teaspoon freshly ground black pepper**

2 **tablespoons olive oil**

½ **pound sliced shiitake mushrooms**

½ **pound sliced white mushrooms**

½ **pound orzo pasta**

¼ **cup freshly grated Parmesan cheese**

1 In a saucepan bring broth, water, and Italian seasoning to boiling; reduce heat and simmer, uncovered.

2 Meanwhile, sprinkle chicken with salt and pepper. In a 12-inch skillet heat 1 tablespoon of the oil over high heat. Add chicken and cook for 1½ minutes on each side or until brown. Use a slotted spoon to transfer chicken to a bowl.

3 Add the remaining 1 tablespoon oil to the skillet. Add mushrooms; cook, covered, for 2 minutes or until softened. Add orzo and cook for 1 minute or until lightly toasted. Set 1 cup hot broth aside in a glass measure. Gradually add remaining broth to pasta, 1 cup at a time, every 2 to 3 minutes, stirring occasionally. (Mixture will be soupy.) Add chicken and reserved 1 cup broth and cook for 2 to 4 minutes more or until thickened. Stir in Parmesan.

Nutrition Facts per serving: 421 cal., 15 g total fat (3 g sat. fat), 50 mg chol., 1,002 mg sodium, 46 g carbo., 3 g fiber, 26 g pro. **Daily Values:** 2% vit. A, 3% vit. C, 11% calcium, 17% iron

ROASTED ASPARAGUS AND RED PEPPERS

Though you can make this vivid vegetable dish any time of year, it's best in the spring when asparagus is in season. Choose slender stalks with tightly closed tips, and be sure not to overcook them.

Prep: 20 minutes   **Bake:** 10 minutes   **Stand:** 20 minutes   **Oven:** 400°F   **Makes:** 4 servings

1 **medium red sweet pepper**	1 **pound fresh asparagus spears, trimmed**
2 **tablespoons olive oil**	2 **tablespoons shredded Parmesan cheese**
1 **teaspoon snipped fresh thyme**	2 **tablespoons snipped fresh parsley**
¼ **teaspoon salt**	**Olive oil (optional)**
¼ **teaspoon freshly ground black pepper**	**Cracked black pepper (optional)**

1 Halve sweet pepper lengthwise; discard stem, membranes, and seeds. Place sweet pepper, cut side down, on a foil-lined baking sheet. Broil 4 to 5 inches from heat for 8 to 10 minutes or until blackened and blistered. Carefully bring foil up and around pepper halves to enclose. Let stand about 20 minutes or until cool enough to handle. Peel skin off sweet pepper. Cut pepper into ½-inch strips; set aside.

2 Combine oil, thyme, salt, and ground pepper; pour over asparagus spears. Toss lightly to coat. Arrange spears in a single layer in a 15×10×1-inch baking pan. Bake, uncovered, in a 400° oven for 10 to 12 minutes or until light brown and tender, turning asparagus once.

3 On a warm serving platter arrange asparagus spears and sweet pepper strips. Combine Parmesan and parsley. Sprinkle mixture over vegetables. If desired, drizzle with olive oil and sprinkle with cracked black pepper. Serve immediately.

Nutrition Facts per serving: 157 cal., 11 g total fat (3 g sat. fat), 12 mg chol., 440 mg sodium, 4 g carbo., 1 g fiber, 8 g pro.
Daily Values: 39% vit. A, 120% vit. C, 23% calcium, 6% iron

Roasted peppers on call: Use roasted sweet peppers in a variety of ways. Add slices of them to soups or chili, puree them for use in pasta sauces, blend them with mayonnaise for a quick dip, or drizzle them with olive oil and balsamic vinegar and top toasted baguette slices. To make sure you always have some on hand, roast a supply when peppers are plentiful and store them in your freezer.

To freeze roasted peppers, place pieces between sheets of waxed paper. Place them in a resealable plastic freezer bag and freeze up to 3 months. To use, thaw at room temperature about 30 minutes. (Or after roasting, place the peppers in a little olive oil in an airtight container and refrigerate for up to 1 week.)

LEMON ICE CREAM

If opera is the favored music of Italian culture, gelato, or Italian ice cream, is the favored treat. Enjoy it as the Italians do, on a warm summer evening while strolling through the neighborhood. A sweet syrup gives this version its refreshing punch.

Prep: 15 minutes   **Chill:** 4 hours   **Freeze:** 2 hours   **Makes:** about 1 quart (8 servings)

4 **large lemons**	$\frac{2}{3}$ **cup freshly squeezed lemon juice**
1$\frac{1}{2}$ **cups water**	$\frac{2}{3}$ **cup whipping cream**
1$\frac{1}{4}$ **cups sugar**	

1 Use a vegetable peeler to remove long, thin strips of lemon peel, being careful not to get any of the white pith; measure $\frac{1}{2}$ cup. Bring water, lemon peel, sugar, and lemon juice to boiling. Boil, uncovered, for 2 minutes. Strain mixture to remove peels; discard peels. Pour lemon mixture into a medium bowl and chill at least 4 hours or up to 24 hours.

2 Add whipping cream and mix well.

3 Pour mixture into a 1$\frac{1}{2}$-quart ice cream maker and freeze according to the manufacturer's instructions. Transfer to a tightly covered nonmetal container; freeze at least 2 hours before serving. Store in freezer for up to 1 week.

Nutrition Facts per serving: 190 cal., 7 g total fat (4 g sat. fat), 27 mg chol., 9 mg sodium, 32 g carbo., 0 g fiber, 0 g pro.
Daily Values: 6% vit. A, 16% vit. C, 2% calcium

MENU:

Italian Salad
w/Garlic Polenta
Croutons
Creamy Tomato
Sauce
Gnocchi Focaccia
Nonna's Chocolate
Cookies

ITALIAN SALAD WITH GARLIC POLENTA CROUTONS

Crusty on the outside and creamy and warm on the inside, the polenta croutons make a good-for-you salad of vegetables and greens tastier than ever.

Prep: 20 minutes   **Bake:** 15 minutes   **Oven:** 425°F   **Makes:** 4 servings

- ½ of a 16-ounce tube refrigerated cooked polenta or 8 ounces leftover polenta
- 1 tablespoon olive oil
- ½ teaspoon garlic-pepper seasoning
- 6 cups torn romaine or torn mixed greens

- ½ of a 7-ounce jar roasted red sweet peppers, drained and cut up (½ cup)
- ½ cup chopped tomato
- ⅓ cup sliced pitted ripe olives
- 2 tablespoons grated Parmesan cheese
- ¼ cup bottled Italian salad dressing

1 Cut polenta into ¾-inch cubes; toss with oil and sprinkle with garlic-pepper seasoning. Spread cubes in a greased shallow baking pan. Bake in a 425° oven for 15 to 20 minutes or until golden, turning once.

2 Meanwhile, in a bowl toss together romaine, roasted sweet peppers, tomato, and olives. Divide salad mixture among 4 salad plates. Top salads with warm polenta croutons; sprinkle with Parmesan cheese. Serve with Italian salad dressing.

Nutrition Facts per serving: 199 cal., 13 g total fat (2 g sat. fat), 3 mg chol., 515 mg sodium, 18 g carbo., 4 g fiber, 5 g pro.
Daily Values: 130% vit. C, 7% calcium, 10% iron

CREAMY TOMATO SAUCE

Italian bacon, pancetta, is salted and cured but not smoked like American bacon. It comes in a roll convenient for slicing as thin as you'd like. If you can't find it at your grocery store, check local Italian markets or delicatessens.

Prep: 20 minutes   **Cook:** 16 minutes   **Makes:** 4 servings

   3 ounces pancetta or bacon, finely chopped
   2 cups sliced fresh mushrooms
   ½ cup pine nuts
   1 tablespoon butter or margarine
   1½ cups heavy cream
   ¼ teaspoon coarsely ground black pepper
   2 medium tomatoes or 4 roma tomatoes, peeled, seeded, and chopped (about 1¾ cups)

   1 recipe Gnocchi (see recipe, page 76)
   ½ cup freshly grated Parmesan cheese
      Coarsely ground black pepper (optional)
      Freshly grated Parmesan cheese (optional)

1 In a large skillet cook and stir pancetta just until golden. Remove from skillet; drain off fat.

2 In the same skillet cook mushrooms and pine nuts in hot butter until mushrooms are tender and pine nuts are golden. Return pancetta to skillet. Stir in the heavy cream and the ¼ teaspoon pepper. Bring to boiling; reduce heat. Boil gently, uncovered, over medium heat about 7 minutes over medium heat or until mixture thickens slightly. Stir in chopped tomatoes.

3 Toss hot cooked gnocchi with the ½ cup Parmesan cheese. Add to tomato mixture; toss lightly to coat. If desired, sprinkle with additional pepper and cheese.

Nutrition Facts per serving (with gnocchi): 771 cal., 55 g total fat (27 g sat. fat), 197 mg chol., 964 mg sodium, 55 g carbo., 3 g fiber, 22 g pro. **Daily Values:** 39% vit. A, 53% vit. C, 23% calcium, 29% iron

GNOCCHI

The low moisture content of russet potatoes, also known as baking potatoes, ensures the light texture of these small potato dumplings. If the gnocchi flatten as you create their distinctive grooves, simply plump them up with your fingers.

Prep: 45 minutes **Bake:** 40 minutes **Oven:** 425°F **Cool:** 1 hour **Cook:** 3 minutes per batch
Makes: 6 servings

1½ **pounds russet potatoes**
1 **egg, beaten**
1 **teaspoon salt**

1 **to 1¼ cups all-purpose flour**
1 **recipe Creamy Tomato Sauce (optional)**
 (see recipe, page 75)

1 Prick the potatoes with a fork. Bake in a 425° oven for 40 to 60 minutes or until tender. Hold hot potatoes with an oven mitt or folded kitchen towel and using a paring knife, scrape skin from the potatoes. (Tip: The hotter the potatoes when they are peeled and pressed through a ricer, the lighter the gnocchi.) Press the peeled hot potatoes through a food mill or ricer into a large bowl. Let the potatoes cool completely.

2 In a small bowl combine egg and salt. Make a well in center of the riced potatoes. Add egg mixture; toss to distribute egg mixture. Stir in 1 cup of the flour; do not overwork dough. Working on a floured surface, knead in enough remaining flour to make a soft smooth dough that is slightly sticky. (If you overwork the dough, it will become very sticky and you will end up with gnocchi that are heavy.) Divide dough into 4 portions. (Tip: Wash your hands and clean the work surface as necessary to keep dough from sticking to your hands or work surface.)

3 Dust the work surface with flour. (Keep the flour handy throughout the rolling and handling process.) Roll dough into logs that are ¾ inch wide. Slice into ½-inch pieces. Gently roll each piece of dough into a ball. Roll dough balls over a lightly floured gnocchi paddle or the tines of a fork to create an oval shape with grooves on one side.

4 Bring a large amount of lightly salted water to boiling in a 5- to 6-quart Dutch oven. Add half of the gnocchi, a few at a time. Stir gently to keep gnocchi from sticking together. Cook about 3 minutes or until gnocchi rise to the top. Using a slotted spoon, remove gnocchi from boiling water to a bowl. (Test gnocchi. If they are floury, cook an additional 10 seconds after they rise to the top.) Repeat with remaining gnocchi. If desired, toss with warm Creamy Tomato Sauce.

Nutrition Facts per serving (gnocchi only): 149 cal., 1 g total fat (0 g sat. fat), 35 mg chol., 403 mg sodium, 30 g carbo., 1 g fiber, 4 g pro. **Daily Values:** 1% vit. A, 21% vit. C, 1% calcium, 9% iron

Squeezing the cooked potatoes through a ricer helps give the gnocchi the lightest texture.

With your thumb, roll gnocchi on a ridged board. Finish with a slight indent, making a "dimple."

FOCACCIA

For a crisper crust and a slightly lighter texture, bake this flatbread on a baking stone. If you don't have a baking stone, shape the dough into a round mound, place it on a greased baking sheet, and bake it on the sheet.

Prep: 30 minutes   **Stand:** Overnight   **Rise:** 1 hour   **Rest:** 30 minutes   **Bake:** 15 minutes
Oven: 475°F   **Makes:** 12 servings

4 to 4¼ cups all-purpose flour	2 teaspoons salt
½ cup warm water (105°F to 115°F)	1 tablespoon olive oil
1 teaspoon active dry yeast	Coarse salt
1 cup warm water (105°F to 115°F)	

1 For the sponge, in a large bowl combine ½ cup of the flour, the ½ cup warm water, and the yeast. Beat with a wooden spoon until smooth. Cover loosely with plastic wrap. Let sponge stand overnight at room temperature to ferment.

2 Gradually stir in the 1 cup warm water, the 2 teaspoons salt, and just enough of the remaining flour to make a dough that pulls away from the sides of the bowl. Turn dough out onto a lightly floured surface. Knead in enough of the remaining flour to make a stiff dough that is smooth and elastic (8 to 10 minutes total). Place dough in a lightly greased bowl, turning once. Cover; let rise in a warm place until doubled (about 1 hour).

3 Turn dough out onto a floured baking sheet. Place an extra-large bowl upside down over the dough to cover; let rest 30 minutes. Meanwhile, preheat the oven and a baking stone to 475°. On the baking sheet, shape dough into a circle about 11 inches in diameter by pulling and pressing with your fingertips. (Don't stretch dough too roughly or it will deflate; you want to keep air bubbles intact.)

4 Dust your fingers with flour and press into dough to make ½-inch-deep indentations spaced about 2 inches apart. Brush dough with olive oil; sprinkle lightly with coarse salt. Carefully slide focaccia from floured baking sheet to the preheated baking stone.

5 Bake for 15 to 20 minutes or until golden, checking after 8 minutes and popping any large air bubbles with a sharp knife. Remove focaccia from baking stone with large spatulas. Cool on a wire rack about 15 minutes. Serve warm.

Herbed Focaccia: Prepare as above, adding 2 teaspoons snipped fresh rosemary with the warm water, salt, and flour in Step 2.

Nutrition Facts per serving for plain or herbed variation: 151 cal., 1 g total fat (0 g sat. fat), 0 mg chol., 583 mg sodium, 29 g carbo., 1 g fiber, 4 g pro. **Daily Values:** 1% calcium, 10% iron

NONNA'S CHOCOLATE COOKIES

Nonna means grandmother in Italian, and if you want these cookies to live up to Nonna's good name, offer a plateful with a cup of espresso.

Prep: 35 minutes   **Bake:** 10 minutes per batch   **Oven:** 375°F   **Makes:** 6 dozen cookies

½ cup butter, softened	⅓ cup strawberry jam
¾ cup granulated sugar	¼ cup cream sherry or prune juice
1 teaspoon baking powder	3 cups all-purpose flour
½ teaspoon baking soda	⅓ cup golden raisins
½ teaspoon ground cinnamon	⅓ cup chopped walnuts
¼ teaspoon ground cloves	3 cups sifted powdered sugar
2 eggs	½ teaspoon vanilla
½ cup unsweetened cocoa powder	3 to 4 tablespoons water

1 In a large mixing bowl beat butter with an electric mixer on medium to high speed for 30 seconds. Add granulated sugar, baking powder, baking soda, cinnamon, and cloves; beat until combined. Add eggs; beat until combined. Beat in cocoa powder, jam, and sherry. Beat in as much of the flour as you can with the mixer. Stir in raisins, walnuts, and any remaining flour.

2 Shape dough into 1-inch balls. Place balls 1 inch apart on a lightly greased cookie sheet. Bake in a 375° oven for 10 to 12 minutes or until cookies are firm. Cool on a wire rack.

3 Combine powdered sugar, vanilla, and enough water to make frosting of dipping consistency. Dip cookie tops into frosting. Place on waxed paper until frosting is set.

Nutrition Facts per cookie: 69 cal., 2 g total fat (1 g sat. fat), 9 mg chol., 30 mg sodium, 12 g carbo., 0 g fiber, 1 g pro.
Daily Values: 1% vit. A, 1% calcium, 2% iron

MENU

Italian Country
Bread Soup

Pork & Porcini Bolognese

Oven-Baked Broccoli

Polenta & Plum Cake

ITALIAN COUNTRY BREAD SOUP

Bread-loving cultures, such as the Italian and French, have devised wonderful ways to use day-old or older bread. This tomato and squash zuppa is just one of them. Toasting the bread helps it hold its shape in the soup.

Prep: 20 minutes   **Bake:** 10 minutes   **Oven:** 375°F   **Cook:** 10 minutes   **Makes:** 6 servings

- **8 ounces Italian flatbread (focaccia), cut into ¾-inch cubes (4 cups)**
- **2½ cups chopped zucchini and/or yellow summer squash**
- **¾ cup chopped green sweet pepper**
- **½ cup chopped onion**

- **1 tablespoon olive oil**
- **2 14-ounce cans chicken broth**
- **1 14½-ounce can diced tomatoes with basil, oregano, and garlic, undrained**
- **Finely shredded Parmesan cheese (optional)**

1 Spread bread cubes in a single layer on an ungreased baking sheet. Bake in a 375° oven for 10 to 15 minutes or until lightly toasted.

2 Meanwhile, in a large saucepan cook zucchini and/or yellow squash, sweet pepper, and onion in hot oil for 5 minutes. Stir in broth and undrained tomatoes. Bring to boiling; reduce heat. Simmer, uncovered, about 5 minutes or until vegetables are tender.

3 Ladle soup into bowls. Top each serving with toasted bread cubes and, if desired, Parmesan cheese.

81

Nutrition Facts per serving: 172 cal., 4 g total fat (1 g sat. fat), 9 mg chol., 526 mg sodium, 27 g carbo., 3 g fiber, 8 g pro.
Daily Values: 5% vit. A, 45% vit. C, 8% calcium, 6% iron

PORK AND PORCINI BOLOGNESE

Several years ago, a well-known pasta sauce manufacturer used the phrase "It's in there!" to sell its product. That could be said with all honesty about this delicious sauce, which combines savory Italian sausage, escarole, and lots of woodsy-tasting porcini mushrooms.

Prep: 25 minutes   **Cook:** 20 minutes   **Stand:** 15 minutes   **Makes:** 4 to 6 main-dish servings

8 cups water	⅓ cup dry white wine or water
2¼ teaspoons sea salt	¾ cup beef or veal broth or stock
1 ounce dried porcini mushrooms	½ cup purchased chunky marinara sauce
1 bunch escarole, core removed, or 8 cups fresh spinach	1 tablespoon snipped fresh parsley
12 ounces bulk pork sausage	1 tablespoon olive oil
½ cup chopped onion	¼ teaspoon freshly ground black pepper
1 tablespoon minced fresh garlic (6 cloves)	2 9-ounce packages refrigerated tagliatelle or fettuccine
1 tablespoon snipped fresh sage	⅓ cup coarsely shaved Parmesan cheese

1 In a 4-quart Dutch oven bring the water and 2 teaspoons of the sea salt to boiling. Place mushrooms in a small bowl; add 1 cup of the boiling water. Let stand for 15 minutes. Meanwhile, add escarole to the remaining boiling water. Return water to boiling; immediately drain escarole in a colander and rinse with cold water. Drain well, pressing out excess liquid; coarsely chop escarole and set aside. Drain mushrooms, reserving 2 tablespoons of the liquid. Chop the mushrooms and set mushrooms and liquid aside.

2 In a large skillet cook sausage, onion, garlic, and sage until meat is brown, stirring to break up sausage. Drain off fat. Stir in wine and reserved mushroom liquid. Bring to boiling; reduce heat. Boil gently, uncovered, about 7 minutes or until most of the liquid is evaporated. Add broth, marinara sauce, parsley, oil, pepper, and the remaining ¼ teaspoon sea salt. Bring to boiling; reduce heat. Simmer, uncovered, for 2 minutes.

3 Meanwhile, in the same Dutch oven cook pasta, using fresh water, according to package directions. Reserve ¼ cup pasta water; drain pasta. Add pasta water, mushrooms, and cooked escarole to pork mixture. Heat through; spoon over cooked pasta. Toss before serving. Top with Parmesan.

Nutrition Facts per main-dish serving: 809 cal., 35 g total fat (14 g sat. fat), 192 mg chol., 1,032 mg sodium, 84 g carbo., 8 g fiber, 32 g pro. **Daily Values:** 47% vit. A, 23% vit. C, 21% calcium, 27% iron

OVEN-BAKED BROCCOLI

What cook doesn't welcome an easy vegetable dish? For this one, simply toss the broccoli with some olive oil and sliced leeks, then put it in the oven and bake it for 20 minutes. Stir only once.

Prep: 5 minutes   **Bake:** 20 minutes   **Oven:** 450°F   **Makes:** 4 to 6 servings

- 2 **tablespoons olive oil**
- 4 **cups broccoli florets**
- 1 **cup thinly sliced leeks (about 3 medium)**

- ½ **teaspoon salt**
- ¼ **teaspoon freshly ground black pepper**

1 Add oil to a 2-quart shallow glass baking dish. Heat in a 450° oven for 1 minute. Add broccoli and stir. Cover the baking dish with foil. Return dish to oven and bake for 15 minutes.

2 Add leeks, salt, and pepper to broccoli; toss to coat. Cover dish with foil and continue baking for 5 to 7 minutes more or until broccoli is tender.

Nutrition Facts per serving: 98 cal., 7 g total fat (1 g sat. fat), 0 mg chol., 319 mg sodium, 8 g carbo., 3 g fiber, 3 g pro.
Daily Values: 28% vit. A, 141% vit. C, 6% calcium, 7% iron

POLENTA AND PLUM CAKE

You can use nearly any variety of plum to make this cake, and they'll taste sweeter if they're ripe. Select plums that are free of blemishes and discoloration, and firm but yield slightly to pressure.

Prep: 35 minutes   **Bake:** 1 hour   **Oven:** 350°F   **Cool:** 20 minutes   **Makes:** 10 servings

- 4 plums, pitted and quartered
- ¼ cup packed brown sugar
- 1 cup all-purpose flour
- ½ cup cornmeal
- 1½ teaspoons baking powder
- ⅛ teaspoon salt
- 1 cup butter, softened
- ¾ cup granulated sugar
- 4 egg yolks
- 2 eggs
- 1 teaspoon finely shredded lemon or orange peel
- 1 teaspoon vanilla

1 Lightly grease and flour bottom and sides of a 9-inch springform pan; line with a 9-inch circle of parchment paper. Set aside.

2 Place plums, skin side up, onto parchment. Sprinkle brown sugar over the plums.

3 In a small bowl combine flour, cornmeal, baking powder, and salt; set aside.

4 In a large mixing bowl beat the butter with an electric mixer on medium to high speed for 30 seconds. Add granulated sugar and beat until light. Add egg yolks and eggs, 1 at a time, beating after each addition. Add lemon peel and vanilla; beat until combined. Beat in the flour mixture. Spread batter over plums in pan.

5 Bake in a 350° oven about 1 hour or until a toothpick inserted near center comes out clean (plums will sink as cake bakes). Cool cake in pan on a wire rack for 20 minutes. Remove sides of pan; cool completely. Invert cake onto serving platter and remove parchment.

Nutrition Facts per serving: 393 cal., 23 g total fat (13 g sat. fat), 180 mg chol., 305 mg sodium, 43 g carbo., 1 g fiber, 4 g pro. **Daily Values:** 23% vit. A, 11% vit. C, 7% calcium, 1% iron

Menu

Fresh Mozzarella Salad

Caponatina

Italian Sausages With Polenta

Cannoli

FRESH MOZZARELLA SALAD

At the peak of tomato season, vendors at Italian markets can scarcely keep fresh mozzarella stocked in their coolers. Summer truly is the best time to make this variation of insalata caprese, when tomatoes are juicy and ripe, but if you want to make it during the off-season, ripen your tomatoes in a brown paper bag.

Start to Finish: 20 minutes   **Makes:** 4 servings

- 1 15-ounce can black beans or garbanzo beans, rinsed and drained
- 1 15-ounce can butter beans or Great Northern beans, rinsed and drained
- 1 small cucumber, quartered lengthwise and sliced (1 cup)
- 2 red and/or yellow tomatoes, cut into thin wedges

- ¼ cup thinly sliced green onions
- 1 recipe Basil Dressing or ½ cup bottled oil-and-vinegar salad dressing
- 8 ounces round or log-shape fresh mozzarella cheese or fresh part-skim Scamorza cheese

1 In a large bowl combine black beans, butter beans, cucumber, tomatoes, and green onions.

2 Add Basil Dressing; toss lightly to coat. Cut cheese into thin slices; gently toss with salad mixture. Serve immediately.

Basil Dressing: In a screw-top jar combine ¼ cup red wine vinegar; ¼ cup olive oil or salad oil; 1 tablespoon snipped fresh basil or 1 teaspoon dried basil, crushed; 1 teaspoon Dijon-style mustard; ¼ teaspoon crushed red pepper; and 1 clove garlic, minced. Cover and shake well. (If desired, cover and chill dressing for up to 2 days.) Makes about ½ cup.

Nutrition Facts per serving: 434 cal., 23 g total fat (8 g sat. fat), 32 mg chol., 919 mg sodium, 37 g carbo., 6 g fiber, 27 g pro. **Daily Values:** 24% vit. C, 36% calcium, 24% iron

Storing fresh tomatoes: It's tempting to set underripe fresh tomatoes in the sun to ripen, but doing so causes the tomatoes to become mushy. Instead place them in a brown paper bag or in a fruit-ripening bowl with other fruits and store them at room temperature. Ripe tomatoes yield slightly to pressure when touched.

Once ripe, do not refrigerate tomatoes because they'll lose their flavor and become mushy. Instead store them at room temperature; they'll keep for 2 to 3 days.

If tomato season finds you with more tomatoes than you can use, freeze them in resealable plastic bags. Because frozen tomatoes soften when thawed, they work best in soups, stews, and casseroles.

CAPONATINA

This Sicilian medley, usually served at room temperature, makes a wonderful salad, side dish, or relish. If you're a fan of anchovies, you can chop up a few and toss them into the mix with the tomatoes, olives, and capers.

Prep: 30 minutes   **Stand:** 3 hours   **Cook:** 13 minutes   **Makes:** 6 to 8 servings

1 large (about 1¼ pounds) eggplant, peeled and cut into ½-inch cubes (6 cups cubes)	½ cup chopped onion
	½ cup chopped celery
1 tablespoon salt	⅔ cup pitted green olives, drained and chopped
2 14½-ounce cans Italian-style stewed tomatoes, undrained	¼ cup capers, drained
1 tablespoon cooking oil	1 tablespoon balsamic vinegar

1 Place the eggplant cubes in a colander and sprinkle them with salt. Place a heavy plate or bowl on the eggplant to weigh them down. Let stand for about 3 hours to drain off the excess water. Rinse and drain eggplant. Cut up any large tomato pieces; set aside.

2 In a large nonstick skillet cook the eggplant in hot oil over medium-high heat for 3 to 4 minutes or until golden brown, stirring occasionally. Remove from skillet. Add onion and celery to the skillet. Cook and stir for 5 minutes or until tender. Return the eggplant to the skillet. Stir in undrained tomatoes, olives, and capers; heat to boiling. Reduce heat; simmer, uncovered, for 5 to 10 minutes or until slightly thickened. Stir in vinegar. Serve warm or at room temperature.

Nutrition Facts per serving: 126 cal., 6 g total fat (1 g sat. fat), 1,026 mg sodium, 16 g carbo., 3 g fiber, 2 g pro.
Daily Values: 3% vit. A, 7% vit. C, 6% calcium, 7% iron

ITALIAN SAUSAGES WITH POLENTA

If you prefer your polenta with sauce, Creamy Tomato Sauce (see page 75) is fantastic with this recipe. Round out this simple, hearty meal with a side of escarole quickly sauteed in olive oil and garlic. Stir in a little chicken broth for added flavor.

Start to Finish: 30 minutes   **Makes:** 4 servings

1 **14-ounce can chicken broth**
1 **cup yellow cornmeal**
2½ **cups milk**
¼ **teaspoon freshly ground pepper**

⅓ **cup finely shredded Parmesan cheese**
4 **links Italian sausage (1 pound)**
½ **cup water**

1 For the polenta, in a large saucepan whisk together chicken broth and cornmeal. Whisk in milk and pepper. Cook and stir over medium heat until mixture boils and thickens. Reduce heat to low. Cook, stirring frequently, for 10 minutes or until very thick. Stir in cheese.

2 Meanwhile, brown sausages in a large skillet over medium-high heat. Carefully add water to the skillet. Reduce heat to medium-low. Cook, covered, for 5 minutes. Uncover; cook about 5 minutes more or until liquid evaporates and sausages are done (160°F), turning to brown sausages.

3 Divide polenta among 4 shallow serving bowls. Top polenta with sausages.

Nutrition Facts per serving: 1,052 cal., 66 g total fat (30 g sat. fat), 197 mg chol., 2,481 mg sodium, 37 g carbo., 2 g fiber, 57 g pro. **Daily Values:** 15% vit. A, 6% vit. C, 77% calcium, 15% iron

CANNOLI

When southern Italian immigrants came to America at the turn of the 20th century, they left much behind—but not their craving for the cream-filled pastries called cannoli.

Prep: 1 hour 15 minutes   **Fry:** 1 minute per batch   **Chill:** Up to 24 hours   **Makes:** 18 servings

2½ **cups all-purpose flour**
½ **cup granulated sugar**
⅛ **teaspoon salt**
¼ **cup shortening**
2 **eggs, slightly beaten**
¼ **cup dry white wine or water**
2 **tablespoons honey**

1 **egg white, slightly beaten**
    Cooking oil or shortening for deep-fat frying
1 **recipe Cream Filling**
    Sifted powdered sugar (optional)
    Chopped pistachio nuts (optional)

1 In a medium bowl stir together flour, granulated sugar, and salt. Cut in shortening until mixture resembles coarse crumbs. In a small bowl stir together the eggs, wine, and honey; add to flour mixture. Stir just until mixture forms a ball. Divide dough in half.

2 On a lightly floured surface roll each half of dough into a 16-inch square. Cut each square into sixteen 4-inch squares. Wrap around lightly greased metal cannoli cylinders from corner to corner, or use wooden rods ¾ to 1 inch in diameter. Moisten overlapping dough with egg white; press gently to seal.

3 Heat oil in a deep fryer to 350°F. Fry a few cannoli at a time in hot oil about 1 minute or until golden brown. Carefully and gently lift from hot oil with tongs, draining any oil that is in tube back into pan. Drain cannoli on paper towels until cool enough to handle. Remove cannoli from tubes and cool completely. Fill with Cream Filling. If desired, sprinkle filled cannoli with powdered sugar and chopped pistachios before serving.

Cream Filling: In a medium bowl stir together two 15-ounce containers ricotta cheese, 1⅓ cups sifted powdered sugar, 1 teaspoon vanilla, and ¼ teaspoon ground cinnamon. Cover and chill for up to 24 hours. Use a pastry bag fitted with a large star tip to fill shells. Or spoon filling into a heavy plastic bag; snip a corner from bag and squeeze filling into shells. Makes about 3⅓ cups filling.

Note: You also can purchase cannoli shells in specialty stores and bakeries. Never fill them more than 4 hours before serving. Store unfilled shells in an airtight container for up to 2 days or freeze for up to 2 months.

Nutrition Facts per cannoli: 207 cal., 10 g total fat (3 g sat. fat), 34 mg chol., 72 mg sodium, 21 g carbo., 0 g fiber, 6 g pro. **Daily Values:** 5% vit. A, 13% calcium, 4% iron

Brushing the dough with egg white helps keep it sealed.

Using a pastry bag makes quick work of filling cannoli.

Menu

Fennel & Orange Salad

Risotto with Leeks & Roasted Asparagus

Honey-Baked Pears

FENNEL AND ORANGE SALAD

The sweet, juicy, ruby-fleshed blood orange most commonly found in American supermarkets is the Moro orange. Its skin is solid orange in color or streaked with red like a sunset, hinting at the hue inside.

Start to Finish: 15 minutes   **Makes:** 4 servings

2 medium fennel bulbs

2 medium blood oranges

¼ cup olive oil

2 tablespoons balsamic vinegar

1 tablespoon snipped fresh chervil or ½ teaspoon dried chervil, crushed

Bibb lettuce leaves

1 green onion, sliced

1 Cut off and discard upper stalks of fennel bulbs, reserving some of the feathery leaves, if desired. Cut off a thin slice from base of fennel bulbs. Remove and discard any wilted outer layers. Wash fennel and cut each bulb into ¼-inch slices, discarding core. Set aside.

2 Peel and section the oranges over a large bowl to catch the juice. For dressing, in the same bowl whisk together the juice from the oranges, olive oil, vinegar, and chervil.

3 Line 4 salad plates with lettuce leaves. Arrange the fennel slices and orange sections on the lettuce; sprinkle with green onion. Drizzle dressing over salads. If desired, garnish salads with reserved fennel leaves.

Nutrition Facts per serving: 159 cal., 14 g total fat (2 g sat. fat), 0 mg chol., 31 mg sodium, 10 g carbo., 15 g fiber, 1 g pro.
Daily Values: 41% vit. C, 3% calcium, 2% iron

RISOTTO WITH LEEKS AND ROASTED ASPARAGUS

It doesn't take any special skill to make risotto, only a little patience for stirring. With its high starch content, arborio rice imparts a creamy texture.

Prep: 20 minutes   **Cook:** 25 minutes   **Bake:** 10 minutes   **Oven:** 450°F   **Makes:** 4 servings

¾ **pound asparagus spears, trimmed**
2 **tablespoons olive oil**
   Salt
   Ground black pepper
1½ **cups sliced leeks**
1 **cup uncooked arborio rice**
3 **cups chicken broth**

⅓ **cup freshly grated Parmesan cheese**
2 **tablespoons snipped fresh parsley**
½ **teaspoon finely shredded lemon peel**
1 **tablespoon lemon juice**
¼ **teaspoon freshly ground coarse black pepper**
   Lemon zest (optional)

1 Brush asparagus spears with 1 tablespoon of the olive oil. Arrange spears in a single layer on a baking sheet; sprinkle lightly with salt and pepper. Bake, uncovered, in a 450° oven about 10 minutes or until crisp-tender. When cool enough to handle, cut asparagus into 2-inch pieces; set aside.

2 Meanwhile, in a large saucepan cook leeks in remaining olive oil until tender. Stir in uncooked rice. Cook and stir over medium heat about 5 minutes or until rice begins to turn golden brown.

3 In another saucepan bring broth to boiling; reduce heat and continue simmering broth while making risotto. Slowly add 1 cup of the broth to the rice mixture, stirring constantly. Continue to cook and stir over medium heat until liquid is absorbed. Add another ½ cup of the broth to the rice mixture, stirring constantly. Continue to cook and stir until liquid is absorbed. Continue adding broth, ½ cup at a time, stirring constantly until all the broth has been absorbed. (This should take about 20 minutes.)

4 Stir in roasted asparagus pieces, Parmesan cheese, parsley, lemon peel, lemon juice, and ¼ teaspoon pepper. If desired, top with lemon zest.

Nutrition Facts per serving: 333 cal., 11 g total fat (3 g sat. fat), 7 mg chol., 755 mg sodium, 44 g carbo., 2 g fiber, 13 g pro. **Daily Values:** 4% vit. A, 35% vit. C, 16% calcium, 20% iron

More flavorful rice: Rice dishes make excellent companions to many meat entrées. To boost the flavor of any type of rice, replace the water for making the rice with chicken broth (flavored with roasted garlic or Italian herbs, if you like), beef broth, vegetable broth, or homemade soup stock.

HONEY-BAKED PEARS

The firmer the pear, the better it holds up in the oven. When available, use Bosc pears for this recipe. They're firm enough to keep their shape after being baked and are still tender to the bite. Mascarpone is a super-rich Italian cream cheese that is available at most supermarkets.

Start to Finish: 45 minutes   **Oven:** 450°F   **Makes:** 4 servings

- 3 **tablespoons butter or margarine, cut up**
- 4 **Bosc pears, quartered and seeded**
- ⅓ **cup honey**
- ¼ **cup fresh lemon juice**
- 2 **tablespoons sugar**
- ¼ **cup mascarpone or dairy sour cream**

1 Place the butter in a rectangular 2-quart baking dish and melt in a 450° oven about 2 minutes.

2 Add the pears to the melted butter in the dish and toss lightly to coat. Pour honey and lemon juice over pears; sprinkle with sugar. Bake for 35 minutes or until pears are tender. Serve warm with mascarpone.

Nutrition Facts per serving: 339 cal., 16 g total fat (9 g sat. fat), 42 mg chol., 102 mg sodium, 52 g carbo., 3 g fiber, 4 g pro. **Daily Values:** 8% vit. A, 22% vit. C, 2% calcium, 3% iron

Menu

Marinated Antipasto

Zucchini alla Romana

Chicken Stuffed with
Smoked Mozzarella

Homemade Pesto with
Linguine

Biscotti

Benvenuto!

MARINATED ANTIPASTO

When you're planning a dinner for many guests, you'll appreciate the make-ahead quality of this appetizer. It tastes best when its ingredients have a day or two to absorb the flavors of the marinade.

Prep: 40 minutes   **Stand:** 30 minutes   **Chill:** 24 hours   **Makes:** 12 to 16 servings

- 1 **pound spicy Italian chicken or turkey sausage links**
- ⅓ **cup olive oil**
- 2 **teaspoons finely shredded lemon peel**
- ⅓ **cup lemon juice**
- 2 **tablespoons snipped fresh basil leaves**
- 2 **teaspoons dried Italian seasoning, crushed**

- 2 **cloves garlic, minced**
- 1 **12-ounce jar roasted red sweet peppers, drained**
- 12 **ounces mozzarella cheese, cut into ½-inch cubes**
- 1 **cup pitted kalamata olives**
  Fresh basil sprigs (optional)

1 In a medium skillet over medium heat cook sausage links for 10 minutes or until cooked through, turning frequently to brown evenly. Drain off fat. Remove sausages from heat and allow to cool. Cut into ¼-inch slices and set aside.

2 Meanwhile, for dressing, in a small bowl whisk together olive oil, lemon peel, lemon juice, snipped basil, Italian seasoning, and garlic; set aside. Cut roasted red peppers into bite-size strips.

3 Layer sausage, red pepper strips, cheese, and olives in a 2-quart jar or two 1-quart jars. Stir dressing. Pour dressing into jar(s), cover tightly, and refrigerate for 1 to 2 days. Turn jar(s) upside down occasionally to distribute the dressing.

4 Let stand at room temperature for 30 minutes before serving. Serve in jar, or arrange on a platter and garnish with basil sprigs, if desired.

Nutrition Facts per serving: 222 cal., 16 g total fat (5 g sat. fat), 36 mg chol., 549 mg sodium, 5 g carbo., 1 g fiber, 13 g pro.
Daily Values: 4% vit. A, 91% vit. C, 20% calcium, 8% iron

ZUCCHINI ALLA ROMANA

Whole cloves of garlic, briefly sauteed and then discarded, flavor the oil in which the zucchini cooks. The garlic imparts its flavor and aroma without overwhelming the mild taste of the squash.

Start to Finish: 15 minutes   **Makes:** 6 servings

2 **cloves garlic**

2 **teaspoons olive oil**

4 **cups sliced zucchini (4 to 5 small)**

1 **tablespoon snipped fresh mint or basil, or 1 teaspoon dried mint or basil, crushed**

¼ **teaspoon salt**

   Dash black pepper

2 **tablespoons finely shredded Parmesan or Romano cheese**

1 In a large skillet cook the whole garlic cloves in hot oil until light brown; discard garlic. Add the zucchini, dried mint (if using), salt, and pepper to the oil in the skillet.

2 Cook, uncovered, over medium heat about 5 minutes or until the zucchini is crisp-tender, stirring occasionally. To serve, sprinkle with the Parmesan cheese and fresh mint (if using).

Nutrition Facts per serving: 35 cal., 2 g total fat (1 g sat. fat), 2 mg chol., 125 mg sodium, 3 g carbo., 1 g fiber, 2 g pro.
Daily Values: 6% vit. A, 10% vit. C, 4% calcium, 3% iron

CHICKEN STUFFED WITH SMOKED MOZZARELLA

This recipe requires that you pound the chicken breasts to flatten them, but take care not to pound them so hard that you tear the flesh, making holes through which the delicious filling can escape.

Prep: 40 minutes   **Bake:** 25 minutes   **Oven:** 400°F   **Makes:** 6 servings

- 6 skinless, boneless chicken breast halves (about 1½ pounds total)
- Salt
- Black pepper
- ¼ cup finely chopped shallots or onions
- 1 clove garlic, minced
- 2 teaspoons olive oil
- ½ of a 10-ounce package frozen chopped spinach, thawed and well drained
- 3 tablespoons pine nuts or walnuts, toasted
- ¾ cup shredded smoked mozzarella cheese
- ¼ cup seasoned fine dry bread crumbs
- ¼ cup grated Parmesan cheese
- 1 tablespoon olive oil

1 Place 1 chicken breast half between 2 pieces of plastic wrap. Pound lightly with the flat side of a meat mallet into a rectangle about ⅛ inch thick. Remove plastic wrap. Season with salt and pepper. Repeat process with remaining chicken breast halves.

2 For filling, in a medium skillet cook shallots and garlic in the 2 teaspoons hot oil until tender. Remove from heat; stir in spinach, nuts, and smoked mozzarella.

3 In a shallow bowl combine bread crumbs and Parmesan cheese.

4 Place 2 to 3 tablespoons of filling on each chicken breast. Fold in the bottom and sides; then roll up. Secure with wooden toothpicks.

5 Lightly brush each roll with the 1 tablespoon olive oil; coat with bread crumb mixture. Place rolls, seam side down, in a shallow baking pan. Bake, uncovered, in a 400° oven about 25 minutes or until chicken is tender and no longer pink. Remove toothpicks before serving.

Nutrition Facts per serving: 274 cal., 11 g total fat (3 g sat. fat), 77 mg chol., 368 mg sodium, 6 g carbo., 1 g fiber, 35 g pro.
Daily Values: 39% vit. A, 6% vit. C, 18% calcium, 8% iron

HOMEMADE PESTO WITH LINGUINE

Consider extra pesto a blessing. If you make a large batch and have lots left over, freeze it in ice cube trays and seal the pesto cubes in plastic bags for a great way to keep small amounts on hand. You can toss the cubes with hot pasta or thaw them and stir them into soups, spread them on bread or crackers, spoon them over baked potatoes, or stir them into mayonnaise for chicken or pasta salad.

Start to Finish: 15 minutes   **Makes:** enough pesto for 18 side-dish servings (about ¾ cup pesto total)

¼ cup olive oil or cooking oil

½ cup chopped walnuts and/or pine nuts

2 cups firmly packed fresh basil leaves

½ cup grated Parmesan or Romano cheese

4 cloves garlic, peeled and quartered

¼ teaspoon salt

Black pepper

Cooked linguine

1 In a food processor bowl or blender container combine oil, nuts, basil, cheese, garlic, and salt. Cover and process or blend until nearly smooth, stopping and scraping sides as necessary. Add black pepper to taste. Serve immediately with cooked linguine or divide it into 3 portions. Place each portion in a small airtight container and refrigerate for 1 to 2 days or freeze up to 3 months.

Note: For 6 side-dish servings, cook 6 ounces dried pasta such as linguine, spaghetti, or fettuccine according to package directions. Toss with 1 portion (¼ cup) of the pesto.

Nutrition Facts per serving pesto with pasta: 166 cal., 6 g total fat (1 g sat. fat), 2 mg chol., 74 mg sodium, 22 g carbo., 1 g fiber, 5 g pro. **Daily Values:** 4% vit. A, 2% vit. C, 5% calcium, 6% iron

BISCOTTI

Impress your guests with these crunchy dunking cookies, a classic accompaniment to the thimble-size cups of espresso Italians drink throughout the day. You can better slice them—and better fit baking them into a busy schedule— if you wrap the baked rolls in plastic wrap and let them stand at room temperature overnight.

Prep: 20 minutes   **Bake:** 38 minutes   **Oven:** 375°/325°F   **Cool:** 1 hour   **Makes:** about 40 biscotti

⅔ **cup sugar**	2 **cups sliced almonds**
2 **tablespoons finely shredded lemon peel**	1¾ **cups all-purpose flour**
2 **eggs**	1 **teaspoon baking powder**
½ **cup cooking oil**	¼ **teaspoon baking soda**
1½ **teaspoons vanilla**	¼ **teaspoon salt**

1 In a food processor or medium mixing bowl combine sugar and lemon peel; add eggs. Process or beat with an electric mixer about 30 seconds. Slowly add oil and vanilla and process or beat until combined. Add 1⅔ cups of the sliced almonds and mix until chopped.

2 In a bowl combine flour, baking powder, soda, and salt; gradually add flour mixture to the almond mixture, processing or beating just until combined. With a wooden spoon, stir in remaining ⅓ cup almonds and up to ¼ cup more flour, if needed, to form a soft dough.

3 Divide dough in half; shape each half into a 12-inch roll. Place the rolls on parchment-lined cookie sheets.

4 Bake in a 375° oven for 20 to 25 minutes or until rolls are light brown and a wooden toothpick inserted near center comes out clean (rolls will spread slightly). Cool on cookie sheet for 1 hour. (If desired, wrap cooled rolls in plastic wrap and let stand overnight at room temperature.)

5 Use a serrated knife to diagonally cut each roll into ½-inch slices. Place slices, cut sides down, on lightly buttered cookie sheets. Bake in a 325° oven for 10 minutes. Turn slices over and bake for 8 to 10 minutes more or until dry and crisp (do not overbake). Transfer to a wire rack and let cool.

Nutrition Facts per cookie: 98 cal., 6 g total fat (0 g sat. fat), 10 mg chol., 35 mg sodium, 8 g carbo., 1 g fiber, 2 g pro.
Daily Values: 1% vit. C, 3% calcium, 3% iron

103

*Purchase Italian bread at an Italian bakery or large supermarket.

MINESTRONE

If you count up all the Italian cooks in the world, you'll find an equal number of minestrone, or "big soup," recipes. For additional flavor, stir a spoonful of pesto into each bowl right before serving.

Prep: 25 minutes   **Cook:** 34 minutes   **Makes:** 6 servings

- 1 cup chopped onion or 2 medium leeks, sliced
- ½ cup chopped carrots
- ½ cup chopped celery
- 1 clove garlic, minced
- 2 tablespoons olive oil or cooking oil
- 2 14½-ounce cans chicken broth
- 1 14½-ounce can tomatoes, cut up, undrained
- 1 cup shredded cabbage
- ¾ cup tomato juice

- 1 teaspoon dried basil, crushed
- 1 15-ounce can cannellini or Great Northern beans, rinsed and drained
- 1 medium zucchini, sliced ¼ inch thick
- ½ of a 9-ounce package frozen Italian green beans
- 2 ounces dried spaghetti or linguine, broken (about ½ cup)
- 2 ounces prosciutto or cooked ham, diced
- ¼ cup finely shredded Parmesan cheese

1 In a 4-quart Dutch oven cook onion, carrots, celery, and garlic in hot oil for about 4 minutes or until onion is tender.

2 Stir in the broth, undrained tomatoes, cabbage, tomato juice, and basil. Bring to boiling; reduce heat. Simmer, covered, for 20 minutes.

3 Stir in the cannellini beans, zucchini, green beans, spaghetti, and prosciutto. Return to boiling; reduce heat. Simmer, covered, for 10 to 15 minutes more or until vegetables and pasta are tender. Top each serving with Parmesan cheese.

Nutrition Facts per serving: 323 cal., 10 g total fat (2 g sat. fat), 13 mg chol., 1,665 mg sodium, 50 g carbo., 11 g fiber, 19 g pro. **Daily Values:** 129% vit. A, 164% vit. C, 27% calcium, 28% iron

EGGPLANT AND DRIED TOMATO PASTA

Cooks in Italy rarely use dried tomatoes. In the 1980s and 1990s, it was the phenomenon known as "Cal-Ital" (Italian-inspired California cooking) that popularized these intensely flavored dried fruits.

Prep: 25 minutes   **Roast:** 25 minutes   **Oven:** 425°F   **Makes:** 4 servings

1 medium onion, cut into 8 wedges

2 tablespoons olive oil

1 medium eggplant (about 1 pound), halved lengthwise

6 ounces dried rigatoni, penne, or fusilli pasta

⅓ cup Dried Tomato Pesto

¼ teaspoon coarsely ground pepper

Salt

2 tablespoons crumbled semisoft goat cheese (chèvre) or feta cheese (optional)

Fresh basil (optional)

1 Place onion wedges in a large shallow baking pan; brush with 1 tablespoon of the olive oil. Roast in a 425° oven for 10 minutes; stir. Brush eggplant with remaining olive oil. Place eggplant in pan, cut side down. Roast 15 minutes more or until onion is golden brown and eggplant is tender.

2 Meanwhile, cook pasta according to package directions; drain. Add ⅓ cup Dried Tomato Pesto and the pepper to pasta; toss gently to coat. Transfer pasta to a warm serving dish; keep warm.

3 Cut roasted eggplant into ½-inch slices. Toss eggplant and roasted onion wedges with pasta. Season to taste with salt. If desired, top with cheese and basil.

Dried Tomato Pesto: Drain ¾ cup oil-packed dried tomatoes, reserving oil. Add enough olive oil to measure ½ cup; set aside. Place drained tomatoes, ¼ cup pine nuts or slivered almonds, ¼ cup snipped fresh basil, ½ teaspoon salt, and 8 cloves garlic, chopped, in a food processor bowl. Cover and process until finely chopped. With machine running, gradually add the reserved oil, processing until almost smooth. Divide pesto into thirds. Refrigerate or freeze unused portions. Makes approximately three ⅓-cup portions.

Nutrition Facts per serving: 370 cal., 19 g total fat (3 g sat. fat), 0 mg chol., 112 mg sodium, 43 g carbo., 4 g fiber, 8 g pro.
Daily Values: 16% vit. C, 2% calcium, 16% iron

WALNUT-CAPPUCCINO TORTE

The torte makes up for its use of very little flour with chopped nuts. Its texture is very moist and dense. This mocha-flavored torte gets its double-coffee flavor from coffee crystals and coffee liqueur. Toast the nuts about 10 minutes in a 350°F oven.

Prep: 25 minutes   **Bake:** 40 minutes   **Oven:** 325°F   **Cool:** 2 hours   **Chill:** 4 hours
Makes: 12 to 16 servings

1   8-ounce package semisweet chocolate, cut up
1⅓ cups milk chocolate pieces (8 ounces)
1   cup whipping cream
2   tablespoons instant coffee crystals
5   eggs
¼   cup coffee liqueur or brewed coffee

1   teaspoon vanilla
½   cup all-purpose flour
¼   cup sugar
1   cup chopped toasted walnuts or pecans
    Mocha Cream
    Fresh raspberries (optional)

1 In a medium heavy saucepan heat semisweet and milk chocolates, whipping cream, and coffee crystals over low heat until the chocolate is melted, stirring constantly. Cool to room temperature.

2 Grease and flour the bottom and sides of a 9-inch springform pan; set aside.

3 In a large mixing bowl beat eggs, coffee liqueur, and vanilla with an electric mixer on low speed until well combined. Add flour and sugar. Beat on medium to high speed for 8 minutes. (The batter should be light and slightly thickened.) Stir about one-fourth of the egg mixture into the chocolate mixture. Stir chocolate mixture into the remaining egg mixture. Stir in nuts.

4 Spread batter in prepared pan. Bake in a preheated 325° oven for 40 to 45 minutes or until slightly puffed around the outer edge (center will be slightly soft). Cool in pan on a wire rack for 20 minutes. Loosen and remove sides of pan. Cool completely. Cover and chill for 4 to 24 hours.

5 To serve, let the torte stand at room temperature for 30 minutes. Top with Mocha Cream. If desired, serve with raspberries.

Mocha Cream: In a chilled small mixing bowl beat ½ cup whipping cream and 2 tablespoons coffee liqueur with an electric mixer on medium-high speed just until soft peaks form.

Nutrition Facts per serving: 462 cal., 32 g total fat (12 g sat. fat), 134 mg chol., 56 mg sodium, 35 g carbo., 3 g fiber, 8 g pro.
Daily Values: 12% vit. A, 1% vit. C, 8% calcium, 11% iron

Mexican

The cheese-smothered burritos, tacos, and enchiladas that Americans devour with the same enthusiasm as hamburgers and pizza represent only the "fast-food" version of this colorful, diverse, and energetic cuisine. The influences of Mexican cooking on American soil go back centuries. After all, Texas, New Mexico, and Arizona were part of Mexico until the United States won the Mexican War in 1848. Spanish, Mexican, native Indian, and Anglo cultures all contributed ingredients, techniques, and foods that make up the dishes of the Southwest. Mexican fare has graced the tables of the border states for centuries, but it is the flood of Mexican immigrants who have crossed the border since 1900—due to Mexico's political unrest and poverty—that has helped spread this intriguing cuisine nationwide. Currently 60 percent of the Hispanic/Latino population in the United States is Mexican-American.

Today it would be difficult to find many Americans who have never dined Mexican. In the United States, the sale of salsa exceeds that of catsup, and tacos and nachos grace more menus than do hot dogs. Moreover, if you've had a cup of cocoa, corn on the cob, pumpkin bread, or vanilla ice cream, Mexico has influenced you. Even at the highest levels of cooking, Mexican cuisine continues to inspire. A new generation of American chefs frequently incorporates Mexican ingredients and techniques into the elaborate dishes they prepare in fine restaurants.

While its slower pace of midday siestas with lingering meals hasn't penetrated the fast-moving culture, Mexico's love of a good celebration such as *Cinco de Mayo,* wildly colorful art and textiles, tequila, lime-topped bottles of beer, and dishes enlivened with chile peppers all add spice to American life.

avocado

serrano and chiles de arbol

Mexican chocolate

clockwise from top: cotija, enchilado, añejo, del caribe cheeses

pumpkin seeds, or *pepitas*

jalapeño and fresno chiles

clockwise from upper left: chipotle, ancho, arbol, cascabel, pequin, New Mexico dried chiles

tomatillos

corn husks

habañero, poblano, and New Mexico chiles

If there is any rival to Italian food as America's best-loved imported cuisine, it might be Mexican cooking. And of all ingredients central to Mexican cuisine, none are more symbolic of its hearty, rustic charm than corn and chile peppers.

The cultivation of **corn** by the Aztecs was a major contribution to the feeding of the world, as it has become the third most important food crop behind wheat and rice. Seven- to seventy-thousand-year-old samples of the predecessors of the modern corn grown and eaten today have been found at Mexican archaeological sites, indicating that this food crop has been grown and eaten by man for a very long time.

In Mexican cooking, corn is indispensable. From corn tortillas, which constitute the daily bread of many people, to tamales (in which even the husk is often used), sopes, tacos, and enchiladas, it is impossible to think of Mexican cooking without considering corn.

Interestingly, the other indispensable element of Mexican cuisine, the **chile pepper,** has a very long history in Mexico too—chiles have most likely been eaten there since approximately 7000 B.C. and cultivated in Mexico since 3500 B.C. Much later, chiles became signature elements in other cuisines, notably in Thai, Indian, and other Asian cuisines, and even in Europe, where milder forms, such as the pepper used in paprika, have helped define entire cuisines (Hungarian). As the birthplace of the chile, Mexico is also home to a multitude of varieties—more than 100—each with particular flavors and aromas desired by cooks for specific culinary uses. Many chiles are used in both fresh and dry forms, and fresh and dry versions often have different names and applications. For example, the fresh green jalapeño is often pickled and served as a condiment or relish, while its dried and smoked form, the chipotle, adds smokiness and searing heat to sauces.

Menu

Chunky Guacamole

Tortilla Chips*

Shredded Savory
Pork Filling

Shredded Pork Tacos

Flan

*purchased item.

CHUNKY GUACAMOLE

If you love guacamole on tortilla chips, try it on grilled sandwiches and alongside grilled meats and poultry.

Prep: 20 minutes   **Chill:** 1 hour   **Makes:** 2 cups (sixteen 2-tablespoon servings)

2 medium roma tomatoes, seeded and cut up

¼ of a small red onion, cut up

1 or 2 cloves garlic, peeled and halved

2 tablespoons lime juice

1 tablespoon olive oil

¼ teaspoon salt

⅛ teaspoon black pepper

2 ripe avocados, seeded, peeled, and cut up

Tortilla chips

1 In a food processor bowl combine roma tomatoes, red onion, garlic, lime juice, olive oil, salt, and pepper.

2 Cover and process with several on-off pulses until mixture is coarsely chopped.

3 Add avocados. Cover and process with on-off pulses just until mixture is chopped. Spoon into a serving bowl and cover the surface with plastic wrap. Chill for up to 1 hour. Serve with tortilla chips.

Nutrition Facts per 2-tablespoon serving: 48 cal., 5 g total fat (1 g sat. fat), 0 mg chol., 39 mg sodium, 3 g carbo., 1 g fiber, 1 g pro. **Daily Values:** 4% vit. A, 7% vit. C, 2% iron

115

Flavor tweaks: Go a step beyond simple guacamole by stirring in additional ingredients before chilling. Choose one or more of the following: 1 fresh green chile or jalapeño pepper, seeded and chopped; ¼ cup dairy sour cream; ¼ cup snipped fresh cilantro; ¼ to ½ teaspoon ground cumin; or ⅛ to ¼ teaspoon ground red pepper.

SHREDDED SAVORY PORK FILLING

Mexican cooks generally like their meats shredded, not ground, after they've been cooked with lots of onions, garlic, chiles, herbs, and spices. Though the northern part of Mexico—particularly the state of Sonora—is known for dishes made with beef, Mexicans eat more pork than any other meat.

Prep: 15 minutes   **Cook:** 2½ hours   **Makes:** 8 servings (about 3 cups cooked meat)

- 1 **2-pound boneless pork blade roast**
- 2 **large onions, quartered**
- 3 **fresh jalapeño peppers, cut up***
- 8 **cloves garlic, minced**
- 2 **teaspoons ground coriander**
- 2 **teaspoons ground cumin**
- 2 **teaspoons dried oregano, crushed**
- ½ **teaspoon salt**
- ½ **teaspoon ground black pepper**

1 Trim fat from meat. Place roast in a large saucepan or Dutch oven; add enough water to nearly cover. Stir in onions, cut-up jalapeño peppers, garlic, ground coriander, cumin, oregano, salt, and black pepper. Bring to boiling. Reduce heat and simmer, covered, for 2½ to 3 hours or until very tender.

2 Remove meat from liquid with a slotted spoon; discard cooking liquid. When cool enough to handle, shred the meat, pulling through it with 2 forks in opposite directions. Use as a filling for tamales or tacos.

Nutrition Facts per serving: 192 cal., 9 g total fat (3 g sat. fat), 46 mg chol., 227 mg sodium, 4 g carbo., 1 g fiber, 23 g pro.
Daily Values: 1% vit. A, 9% vit. C, 5% calcium, 10% iron

*Note: Because hot peppers, such as habañeros and other chiles, contain volatile oils that can burn your skin and eyes, avoid direct contact with them as much as possible. When working with chile peppers, wear plastic or rubber gloves. If your bare hands do touch the peppers, wash your hands well with soap and water.

CHRISTMAS EVE SALAD

This jewel-tone salad features tropical and citrus fruits native to Mexico and is traditionally served with turkey—another food native to Mexico—after Midnight Mass on Christmas Eve.

Prep: 30 minutes   **Chill:** 2 hours   **Makes:** 6 side-dish servings

⅓ cup olive oil

3 tablespoons vinegar

2 tablespoons lime juice

2 tablespoons sugar

2 medium oranges

2 cups cubed fresh pineapple or one 20-ounce can juice-packed pineapple chunks, drained

1 large apple, cored and sliced

Romaine lettuce leaves

4 cups shredded leaf lettuce

1 medium banana, sliced

1 16-ounce can beets, rinsed, drained, and sliced

1 cup jicama, cut into thin bite-size strips

½ cup pine nuts or peanuts

½ cup finely chopped red onion or pomegranate seeds

1 For dressing, in a screw-top jar combine olive oil, vinegar, lime juice, and sugar. Cover and shake well. Chill for 2 to 24 hours.

2 Peel and section the oranges over a large bowl to catch the juice. Add orange sections, pineapple, and apple slices to the bowl. Toss to coat all of the fruit with orange juice. Cover and chill for 2 to 24 hours.

3 To serve, line 6 salad plates with romaine lettuce leaves. Top with shredded lettuce. Add banana slices to the fruit mixture; toss to coat bananas with juice. Drain the juice from the fruit mixture. Arrange the fruit mixture, beets, and jicama on the salad plates. Sprinkle each serving with pine nuts and onion. Shake the salad dressing and pour some over each salad.

Nutrition Facts per serving: 313 cal., 19 g total fat (3 g sat. fat), 0 mg chol., 209 mg sodium, 37 g carbo., 5 g fiber, 5 g pro.
Daily Values: 83% vit. C, 5% calcium, 19% iron

TAMALES

In Mexico, tamales take their rightful place on nearly any fiesta table.

Prep: 2 hours **Cook:** 2¼ hours. **Stand:** 1 hour **Makes:** 36 tamales

1½ pounds boneless pork shoulder or pork butt, cut into chunks
1 small onion, quartered
1 clove garlic, crushed
3 teaspoons salt
½ teaspoon whole black peppercorns
4 dried New Mexico peppers
2 dried ancho peppers
3 cups boiling water

½ teaspoon cumin seeds, toasted*
2 cloves garlic
1 cup lard or shortening
2 teaspoons baking powder
4 cups corn tortilla flour
½ cup ground blanched almonds
36 dried corn husks (about 8 inches long and 6 inches wide at the top)

1 For filling, combine pork, onion, 1 clove crushed garlic, ½ teaspoon of the salt, and whole black peppercorns in a 4-quart Dutch oven. Add enough water to cover (about 6 cups). Bring to boiling; reduce heat. Cover and simmer over medium-low heat for 1½ hours or until meat is very tender. Remove meat from broth. Let meat and broth cool. Remove any fat and discard; shred the meat. Strain broth and reserve 2 cups for preparing dough.

2 For sauce, toast New Mexico and ancho peppers in a dry skillet over medium heat for 4 to 5 minutes, turning frequently, until they have a toasted aroma. Let cool. Wearing disposable plastic gloves or small plastic bags, remove stems, seeds, and ribs from peppers. Tear peppers into pieces and place in a bowl. Cover with the boiling water and let stand for 30 to 60 minutes to soften. Strain soaking liquid through 100-percent-cotton cheesecloth; reserve liquid.

3 Place soaked peppers in a blender container with cumin, 2 cloves garlic, and 1 teaspoon of the remaining salt. Add 1 cup of the soaking liquid; cover and blend until smooth. Transfer to a small saucepan. Simmer, uncovered, over medium heat for 15 to 20 minutes or until reduced to 1⅓ cups. Add pork. Cool completely (about 1 hour). (Filling can be made a day ahead and refrigerated until use.)

4 For dough, beat lard and baking powder with an electric mixer at medium speed for 2 minutes or until smooth. Combine corn tortilla flour, almonds, and the remaining 1½ teaspoons salt. Alternately add flour mixture and reserved pork broth to lard while beating. Mixture should resemble a thick, creamy paste. Meanwhile, soak husks in hot water for 30 minutes or until soft. Drain well; pat dry.

5 To assemble each tamale, starting about 1 inch from the top edge of the husk, spread about 2 tablespoons of dough into a rectangle 3 inches wide and 4 inches long so one of the long sides is at the long edge of the wrapper. Spoon filling down center. Fold the long edge of the wrapper over the filling so it overlaps dough slightly. Roll wrapper around outside of filled dough mixture. Tie ends with strips of corn husk or heavy kitchen string.

6 To steam, stand tamales upright in a steamer basket in a very large Dutch oven. Don't pack them in too tightly, but fill the space. Place at least 1½ inches of water in the bottom of the pan. Bring to boiling; cover. Reduce heat to medium-low. Steam for 45 to 60 minutes. Tamales are done when dough easily pulls away from corn husks and is spongy and well cooked throughout.

*Note: To toast cumin seeds, heat seeds in a dry skillet over medium heat for 1 to 2 minutes or until fragrant. Remove from skillet immediately so they don't burn.

Nutrition Facts per tamale: 142 cal., 8 g total fat (3 g sat. fat), 18 mg chol., 230 mg sodium, 12 g carbo., 2 g fiber, 6 g pro.
Daily Values: 1% vit. C, 5% calcium, 8% iron

FRIJOLES REFRITOS

Frijoles refritos are, simply put, refried beans. Their deeply satisfying creamy texture and smoky flavor belie the simple way they are made. Serve them as a side dish alone—or wrap them in a warm flour tortilla and serve with fresh tomato salsa and rice on the side for a complete meal.

Prep: 20 minutes **Cook:** 2½ hours plus 8 minutes **Stand:** 1 hour
Makes: about 4½ cups (8 side-dish servings)

1 **pound dry pinto beans (about 2⅓ cups)**	¼ **cup bacon drippings**
16 **cups water**	1 **clove garlic, minced**
1 **teaspoon salt**	

1 Rinse beans. In a large saucepan or Dutch oven combine beans and the first 8 cups water. Bring to boiling; reduce heat. Simmer, covered, for 2 minutes. Remove from heat. Cover and let stand for 1 hour. (Or place beans in water in pan. Cover and let soak in a cool place overnight.) Drain and rinse beans.

2 In the same saucepan or Dutch oven combine beans, the remaining 8 cups fresh water, and the salt. Bring to boiling; reduce heat. Simmer, covered, for 2½ to 3 hours or until beans are very tender. Drain beans, reserving liquid.

3 In a large heavy skillet heat bacon drippings. Stir in garlic. Add beans; mash thoroughly with a potato masher. Stir in enough of the cooking liquid (about ½ cup) to make a pastelike mixture. Cook, uncovered, over low heat for 8 to 10 minutes or until thick, stirring often.

Nutrition Facts per serving: 250 cal., 7 g total fat (3 g sat. fat), 6 mg chol., 296 mg sodium, 36 g carbo., 14 g fiber, 12 g pro. **Daily Values:** 5% vit. C, 6% calcium, 15% iron

BISCOCHITOS

A classic at Christmastime throughout Mexico and the Southwest, these anise-flavored biscuity cookies traditionally take the form of birds, flowers, and other fanciful shapes.

Prep: 30 minutes   **Bake:** 9 minutes per batch   **Oven:** 350°F   **Makes:** about 36 (2½-inch) cookies

3 cups all-purpose flour	½ cup granulated sugar
1½ teaspoons anise seeds, crushed	3 tablespoons frozen orange juice concentrate, thawed, or brandy
1 teaspoon baking powder	1 teaspoon vanilla
½ teaspoon salt	Cinnamon sugar (optional)
1¼ cups butter-flavored shortening	Anise seeds, crushed (optional)
1 egg	

1 Lightly grease a cookie sheet; set aside. In a medium bowl stir together the flour, the 1½ teaspoons anise seeds, the baking powder, and salt; set aside.

2 In a large mixing bowl beat shortening with an electric mixer on medium speed until fluffy. Add egg, granulated sugar, orange juice concentrate, and vanilla. Beat until mixture is light. Beat in as much of the flour mixture as you can (dough will be stiff). Use a spoon to stir in the remaining flour mixture. Divide dough in half.

3 Turn dough out onto a lightly floured surface. Use a floured rolling pin to roll half the dough at a time to ¼-inch thickness. Use a 2½-inch cutter to cut dough shapes. If desired, sprinkle cutouts with cinnamon sugar and additional crushed anise seeds. Transfer to prepared cookie sheet.

4 Bake in a 350° oven about 9 minutes or until bottoms are golden. Transfer to a wire rack; cool.

Nutrition Facts per cookie: 112 cal., 7 g total fat (2 g sat. fat), 6 mg chol., 45 mg sodium, 11 g carbo., 0 g fiber, 1 g pro.
Daily Values: 2% vit. A, 4% vit. C, 2% calcium, 3% iron

125

FRESH TOMATO SALSA

Make this version of *salsa fresca* when summer sun lights the sky and farmers' markets are fully stocked with vine-ripened tomatoes. You can make it as hot as you like, depending on the type and quantity of peppers you use.

Prep: 20 minutes   **Chill:** 1 hour   **Makes:** about 3 cups (twelve ¼-cup servings)

1½   cups finely chopped tomatoes
       (3 small)

1   fresh Anaheim pepper, seeded and
       finely chopped, or one 4-ounce can
       diced green chile peppers, drained*

¼   cup chopped green sweet pepper

¼   cup sliced green onions

3   to 4 tablespoons snipped fresh
       cilantro or parsley

2   tablespoons lime juice or lemon juice

1   to 2 fresh jalapeño, serrano, Fresno, or
       banana peppers, seeded and finely
       chopped*

1   clove garlic, minced

⅛   teaspoon salt

⅛   teaspoon black pepper

1 In a medium bowl stir together chopped tomatoes, Anaheim pepper, sweet pepper, green onions, cilantro, lime juice, jalapeño pepper, garlic, salt, and black pepper.**

2 Cover and chill for 1 to 24 hours before serving.

Make-ahead tip: Spoon the salsa into a storage container. Cover and chill for up to 3 days.

Nutrition Facts per tablespoon: 10 cal., 0 g total fat (0 g sat. fat), 0 mg chol., 28 mg sodium, 2 g carbo., 0 g fiber, 1 g pro. **Daily Values:** 12% vit. A, 32% vit. C, 1% calcium, 1% iron

*See note, page 116.

**Note: For a slightly smoother salsa, place 1 cup of the salsa in a food processor bowl or blender container. Cover and process or blend just until smooth. Stir into remaining salsa.

QUESADILLAS

If you ordered a grilled cheese sandwich in Mexico, you'd get a quesadilla. To make this delicious chicken-stuffed version truly authentic, use Chihuahua—similar to a mild cheddar—or asadero or queso quesadilla—both are creamy cheeses from the north of Mexico.

Prep: 20 minutes   **Cook:** 3 minutes per batch   **Oven:** 300°F   **Makes:** 12 servings

 1 medium fresh Anaheim pepper or one 4-ounce can diced green chile peppers, drained*

1½ cups shredded asadero, Chihuahua, queso quesadilla, or Monterey Jack cheese

 6 8-inch flour tortillas

 1 cup shredded cooked chicken

 ½ cup chopped, seeded tomato (1 small)

 3 tablespoons finely chopped green onions (2)

 1 tablespoon snipped fresh cilantro, oregano, or basil

Chunky Guacamole (see recipe, page 115) (optional)

Fresh Tomato Salsa (see recipe, page 127) (optional)

1 If using Anaheim pepper, halve pepper lengthwise; remove seeds and membrane. Cut pepper into thin slivers.

2 Sprinkle ¼ cup of the cheese over half of each tortilla. Sprinkle pepper slivers, chicken, tomato, onions, and cilantro equally over cheese. Fold tortillas in half, pressing gently.

3 In a large skillet or on a griddle cook quesadillas, two at a time, over medium heat for 3 to 4 minutes or until light brown, turning once. Remove quesadillas from skillet and place on a baking sheet. Keep warm in a 300° oven. Repeat with remaining quesadillas.

4 To serve, cut quesadillas in half. If desired, serve with Chunky Guacamole and Fresh Tomato Salsa.

Nutrition Facts per serving: 110 cal., 5 g total fat (3 g sat. fat), 23 mg chol., 212 mg sodium, 8 g carbo., 0 g fiber, 8 g pro.
Daily Values: 2% vit. A, 19% vit. C, 8% calcium, 4% iron

*See note, page 116.

FLOUR TORTILLAS

While corn tortillas are the staple bread in most of Mexico, tortillas made with wheat flour are more common in northern Mexico. Across the border, they're more often made with lard, but vegetable shortening works just as well.

Prep: 45 minutes   **Cook:** 40 seconds per tortilla   **Makes:** twelve 6-inch or eight 8-inch tortillas

2 **cups all-purpose flour**	2 **tablespoons shortening**
1 **teaspoon baking powder**	½ **cup warm water**
½ **teaspoon salt**	

1 In a medium bowl combine flour, baking powder, and salt. Cut in shortening until combined. Gradually add warm water, tossing together until dough can be gathered into a ball (if necessary, add more water, 1 tablespoon at a time). Knead dough 15 to 20 times. Cover and let dough rest for 15 minutes.

2 For 6-inch tortillas, divide dough into 12 equal portions; shape into balls. (For 8-inch tortillas, divide dough into 8 equal portions; shape into balls.) On a lightly floured surface, use a rolling pin to flatten each ball of dough into a 6-inch (or 8-inch) circle.

3 Place tortillas, one at a time, on a medium-hot ungreased skillet or griddle. Cook tortilla 20 to 30 seconds or until puffy. Turn and cook 20 to 30 seconds more or until edges curl slightly. Wrap tortillas in foil.

129

Nutrition Facts per 8-inch tortilla: 133 cal., 3 g total fat (1 g sat. fat), 196 mg sodium, 22 g carbo., 3 g pro. **Daily Values:** 3% calcium, 7% iron

Chili Powder Tortillas: Prepare as above, except add 1 tablespoon ancho chili powder or chili powder to the flour mixture (add more water, if necessary).

FISH TACOS

These grilled fish tacos originated on the Yucatan peninsula of Mexico. Don't marinate the fish any longer than 30 minutes or you'll wind up with seviche, a Latin American appetizer that features raw fish marinated in citrus juice. Nearly any fresh fish will do here, including sea bass, halibut, or tuna.

Prep: 20 minutes　　**Marinate:** 30 minutes　　**Bake:** 10 minutes　　**Broil:** 8 minutes　　**Oven:** 350°F
Makes: 4 servings

1	**pound fresh or frozen firm-fleshed fish fillets (such as orange roughy, salmon, and halibut), cut 1 inch thick**
¼	**cup tequila, lime juice, or lemon juice**
2	**tablespoons lime juice or lemon juice**
1	**fresh jalapeño or serrano pepper, seeded and finely chopped***
¼	**teaspoon ground cumin**
2	**cloves garlic, minced**
24	**4-inch corn tortillas or eight 8-inch flour tortillas**

1½　**cups shredded lettuce**
1　**cup chopped red or green sweet pepper**
1　**medium red onion, halved and thinly sliced**
Snipped fresh cilantro (optional)
Mango or papaya slices (optional)
Salsa (optional)

130

1 Thaw fish, if frozen. Rinse fish; pat dry with paper towels. Place fish in a shallow nonmetal dish.

2 For marinade, in a small bowl stir together tequila, lime juice, jalapeño pepper, cumin, and garlic. Pour marinade over fish. Cover and marinate at room temperature for 30 minutes, turning fish occasionally.

3 Meanwhile, wrap tortillas tightly in foil. Heat in a 350° oven about 10 minutes or until heated through.

4 Drain fish; discard marinade. Pat fish dry with paper towels.

5 Place fish on the greased unheated rack of a broiler pan. Broil 4 inches from the heat for 5 minutes. Using a wide spatula, carefully turn the fish. Broil for 3 to 7 minutes more or just until fish flakes easily when tested with a fork. (Or place fish fillets in a well-greased wire grill basket. Grill on the rack of an uncovered grill directly over medium coals for 8 to 12 minutes or just until fish flakes easily when tested with a fork, turning once.)

6 With a fork, break grilled fish into ½-inch chunks. To assemble tacos, place lettuce in center of each warm tortilla. Divide fish chunks, sweet pepper, and red onion among tortillas. Fold tortillas in half over filling. If desired, serve tacos with cilantro, mango slices, and salsa.

Nutrition Facts per serving: 276 cal., 5 g total fat (1 g sat. fat), 22 mg chol., 314 mg sodium, 34 g carbo., 2 g fiber, 21 g pro. **Daily Values:** 55% vit. A, 128% vit. C, 11% calcium, 14% iron

*See note, page 116.

RICE PUDDING

Rum-soaked raisins give the finished pudding an extra hint of flavor. In the winter, serve this sweet and simple dessert warm; in the summer, serve it chilled.

Prep: 10 minutes   **Cook:** 20 minutes   **Makes:** 3 cups (6 servings)

½ **cup golden raisins**	3 **inches stick cinnamon**
¼ **cup rum (optional)**	¼ **cup sugar**
3 **cups milk**	1 **teaspoon vanilla**
½ **cup long grain rice**	**Ground cinnamon**

1 In a small bowl combine the raisins and rum, if using; set aside.

2 In a heavy medium saucepan combine milk, uncooked rice, and stick cinnamon. Bring to boiling. Reduce heat and simmer, covered, about 20 minutes or until rice is tender. Remove stick cinnamon.

3 Drain raisins; discard rum. Stir raisins, sugar, and vanilla into rice mixture. Sprinkle with ground cinnamon. Serve warm or chilled.

Nutrition Facts per ½-cup serving: 214 cal., 3 g total fat (2 g sat. fat), 10 mg chol., 64 mg sodium, 38 g carbo., 5 g fiber, 6 g pro. **Daily Values:** 5% vit. A, 3% vit. C, 16% calcium, 6% iron

132

Menu

Sopes & Flautas
Chile Colorado
Stuffed Chiles
in Walnut Sauce
Cinnamon Hot Chocolate
Mexican Cookies*

*Purchase Mexican cookies or pastries from a local Mexican
market or by mail order. See Resources, page 279.

SOPES

Made from fried corn masa, these little bean-and-cheese-filled boats are the perfect finger food, which means they're great for cocktail parties. Serve them with margaritas, ice cold cerveza, or Mexican sodas.

Prep: 1 hour   **Cook:** 1 minute per shell   **Chill:** 1 hour   **Makes:** 24 sopes

1½ **cups corn tortilla flour**
3 **tablespoons all-purpose flour**
½ **teaspoon salt**
½ **cup water**
1 **beaten egg**
¼ **cup shortening, melted**

Cooking oil
1 **recipe Black Bean Filling**
   Assorted toppings, such as shredded lettuce, chopped tomatoes, sour cream, Cotija or Monterey Jack cheese, and avocado slices (optional)

1 In a bowl combine tortilla flour, all-purpose flour, and salt. Stir in water and egg. Add shortening; mix well. Knead dough gently until it is moist but holds its shape. Cover and chill for 1 hour.

2 Divide the dough into 24 portions; cover dough to prevent it from drying out. Roll each portion of dough into a ball. On a well-floured surface, pat each ball into a 3-inch round. Form a shell by pinching the edge of the round to make a ridge.

3 In a saucepan or deep skillet heat about ½ inch of cooking oil to 365°F. Fry shells, one or two at a time, about 30 seconds on each side or until crisp. Remove shells with a slotted spoon. Drain shells upside down on paper towels.

4 Fill each shell with Black Bean Filling. If desired, top sopes with assorted toppings.

Black Bean Filling: In a saucepan heat one 15-ounce can black beans, rinsed and drained. Mash beans slightly with a potato masher or fork. Stir in ¼ cup salsa.

Nutrition Facts per sope: 113 cal., 8 g total fat (2 g sat. fat), 11 mg chol., 114 mg sodium, 9 g carbo., 1 g fiber, 3 g pro.
Daily Values: 1% vit. A, 4% calcium, 3% iron

FLAUTAS

In the Spanish language, "flauta" means "flute." It also describes the shape of these chicken- and black-bean-filled flour tortillas, which are crisp-fried and topped with guacamole, salsa, and sour cream.

Prep: 25 minutes   **Cook:** 2 minutes per batch   **Oven:** 350°F/300°F   **Makes:** 6 flautas

6 **10-inch flour tortillas**	**Cooking oil**
½ **cup chopped onion (1 medium)**	3 **cups shredded lettuce**
1 **clove garlic, minced**	**Chunky Guacamole (page 115) (optional)**
1 **teaspoon cooking oil**	**Fresh Tomato Salsa (page 127) (optional)**
2 **cups shredded cooked chicken**	**Dairy sour cream (optional)**
1 **cup canned black beans, rinsed and drained**	
½ **cup salsa**	
2 **tablespoons snipped fresh cilantro or oregano**	

1 Wrap tortillas tightly in foil. Heat in a 350° oven about 10 minutes or until heated through.

2 Meanwhile, for filling, in a large saucepan cook onion and garlic in the 1 teaspoon hot oil until tender. Stir in chicken, black beans, salsa, and cilantro.

3 For each flauta, spoon about ½ cup filling near edge of each warm tortilla. Roll up tortillas as tightly as possible. Secure with wooden toothpicks.

4 In a 12-inch skillet heat 1½ inches of cooking oil to 365°F. Fry flautas, two or three at a time, for 2 to 3 minutes or until crisp and golden brown, turning once. Drain on paper towels. Keep flautas warm in a 300° oven while frying remaining flautas.

5 To serve, remove toothpicks. Place flautas on shredded lettuce. If desired, top with Chunky Guacamole, Fresh Tomato Salsa, and sour cream.

Make-ahead tip: Prepare the filling as directed. Cover and chill for up to 24 hours.

Nutrition Facts per flauta: 348 cal., 17 g total fat (3 g sat. fat), 41 mg chol., 373 mg sodium, 30 g carbo., 3 g fiber, 19 g pro. **Daily Values:** 18% vit. A, 18% vit. C, 9% calcium, 16% iron

CHILE COLORADO

This is the basic red sauce of New Mexico, and it's made with fresh tomatoes, sweet and mild dried ancho chiles, fresh tomatoes, and dried, smoked jalapeños also known as chipotles. Use it to add zest to eggs, enchiladas, tamales, and grilled meats and poultry.

Prep: 1 hour **Cook:** 20 minutes **Makes:** about 2 cups (sixteen 2-tablespoon servings)

- 12 dried ancho chiles or dried mild New Mexico red peppers (4 ounces)*
- 4 dried chipotle chiles or 4 canned chipotle chiles in adobo sauce, rinsed, drained, seeded, and finely chopped*
- 3 cups water
- ½ cup chopped onion (1 medium)
- 1 tablespoon snipped fresh oregano or 1 teaspoon dried oregano, crushed

- 3 cloves garlic, minced
- 1 tablespoon olive oil or cooking oil
- 1½ cups chopped tomatoes (2 medium)
- ¼ teaspoon salt
- ¼ teaspoon ground cumin

1 Cut dried ancho chiles and dried chipotle chiles. Open chiles; discard stems and seeds. Cut chiles into small pieces. Bring water to boiling; remove from heat. Add chiles and let stand for 45 to 60 minutes to soften. Do not drain.

137

2 Meanwhile, in a large skillet cook onion, oregano, and garlic in hot oil for 3 minutes. Remove from heat; set aside.

3 Place half of the undrained dried chiles and half of the chopped tomatoes in a food processor bowl or blender container. Cover and process or blend until nearly smooth. Strain through a fine sieve to remove chile skins and tomato skins and seeds; discard skins and seeds. Repeat blending and straining with remaining chiles and tomatoes. Add strained mixture to onion mixture in skillet along with salt and cumin.

4 Bring to boiling; reduce heat. Simmer, uncovered, for 20 to 25 minutes or to desired consistency.

Make-ahead tip: Spoon sauce into an airtight storage container. Cover and chill for up to 1 week.

Nutrition Facts per 2-tablespoon serving: 53 cal., 2 g total fat (1 g sat. fat), 0 mg chol., 45 mg sodium, 9 g carbo., 3 g fiber, 2 g pro. **Daily Values:** 55% vit. A, 7% vit. C, 2% calcium, 9% iron

*See note, page 116.

STUFFED CHILES IN WALNUT SAUCE

Served on September 15, which is Mexico's Independence Day, this elegant dish is famous not only for its special-occasion flavors but also because it features the colors of the Mexican flag: red, green, and white.

Prep: 30 minutes   **Bake:** 20 minutes   **Oven:** 350°F   **Makes:** 6 (1-cup) servings

1 **pound ground pork or ground raw turkey or chicken**	¼ **teaspoon ground cumin**
⅓ **cup chopped onion (1 small)**	¼ **cup slivered almonds, toasted**
1 **clove garlic, minced**	6 **large fresh poblano peppers or 3 small green sweet peppers**
2 **cups chopped peeled apple and/or pear (2 large)**	½ **cup walnuts**
1 **8-ounce can tomato sauce**	1 **3-ounce package cream cheese, cut up**
¼ **cup raisins**	⅓ **cup milk**
½ **teaspoon salt**	¼ **teaspoon ground cinnamon**
¼ **teaspoon ground cinnamon**	⅛ **teaspoon salt**
	Chile Colorado (page 137) (optional)

1 For filling, in a large skillet cook ground pork, onion, and garlic until meat is brown and onion is tender. Drain off fat. Stir in chopped apple, tomato sauce, raisins, ½ teaspoon salt, ¼ teaspoon cinnamon, and cumin. Bring to boiling. Reduce heat and simmer, covered, for 10 minutes. Stir in almonds.

2 Meanwhile, cut a lengthwise slit in a side of each poblano pepper and remove seeds and membrane. In a saucepan cook poblano peppers or sweet peppers in boiling water about 5 minutes or until crisp-tender. Drain the peppers well.

3 Spoon the meat mixture into the peppers. Place the stuffed peppers in a 2-quart rectangular baking dish. Bake in a 350° oven about 20 minutes or until heated through.

4 Meanwhile, for the sauce, in a blender container or food processor bowl combine walnuts, cream cheese, milk, ¼ teaspoon cinnamon, and ⅛ teaspoon salt. Cover and blend or process until smooth.

5 To serve, spoon walnut sauce and, if desired, Chile Colorado onto serving plates. Place stuffed peppers on top of the sauces.

Make-ahead tip: Cover and chill the filled peppers and the sauce separately for up to 24 hours. To serve, bake the peppers for 25 to 30 minutes or until heated through. Let the sauce stand at room temperature while peppers bake.

Nutrition Facts per serving: 337 cal., 20 g total fat (6 g sat. fat), 52 mg chol., 500 mg sodium, 25 g carbo., 3 g fiber, 16 g pro. **Daily Values:** 23% vit. A, 519% vit. C, 9% calcium, 25% iron

CINNAMON HOT CHOCOLATE

To make this recipe the authentic way, buy Mexican chocolate disks, which are flavored with sugar, cinnamon, and/or ground almonds. Break the disks into wedges, melt them in hot milk, then beat them to a froth with a *molinillo*, a traditional carved wooden beater.

Prep: 10 minutes   **Cook:** 10 minutes   **Makes:** 4 (8-ounce) servings

3 ounces semisweet chocolate, cut up	½ teaspoon vanilla
1 tablespoon sugar	Few drops almond extract
½ to 1 teaspoon ground cinnamon	Whipped cream (optional)
4 cups milk	

1 Combine chocolate, sugar, and cinnamon in a blender container or food processor bowl. Cover and blend or process until finely ground.

2 In a large saucepan combine the ground chocolate mixture and milk. Cook and stir over low heat about 10 minutes or until chocolate is melted. Remove saucepan from heat and stir in vanilla and almond extract. Beat with a rotary beater or Mexican molinillo until very frothy. Serve in mugs. If desired, top each serving with whipped cream.

Nutrition Facts per serving: 240 cal., 11 g total fat (6 g sat. fat), 18 mg chol., 122 mg sodium, 22 g carbo., 3 g fiber, 8 g pro. **Daily Values:** 4% vit. C, 30% calcium, 1% iron

139

MENU
Salsa verde
Tortilla Chips*
Chicken & Shrimp Tortilla Soup
Bolillos
Bread Pudding

SALSA VERDE

Blistering the tomatillos under the broiler concentrates their natural sweetness and intensifies their flavor. Tomatillos are called *tomato verde* (green tomato) in Mexico. Their flavor is slightly acidic and citrusy.

Prep: 20 minutes   **Broil:** 7 minutes   **Stand:** 10 minutes   **Makes:** 1½ cups (six ¼-cup servings)

¾ **pound fresh tomatillos, husks removed, or one 11-ounce can tomatillos, rinsed and drained**

1 **serrano chile***

1 **poblano chile**

1 **teaspoon minced garlic**

1 **teaspoon salt (½ teaspoon if using canned tomatillos)**

¼ **teaspoon sugar**

½ **cup water**

2 **tablespoons chopped onion**

2 **tablespoons snipped fresh cilantro**

1 Arrange tomatillos and serrano and poblano chiles on a foil-lined broiler pan. Broil until charred, about 7 to 8 minutes. Wrap in aluminum foil; let stand for 10 minutes.

2 Peel and seed chiles. In a food processor bowl combine tomatillos, chiles, garlic, salt, and sugar; process until chopped. Stir in water, chopped onion, and cilantro.

141

Nutrition Facts per ¼-cup serving: 24 cal., 0 g total fat (0 g sat. fat), 0 mg chol., 390 mg sodium, 5 g carbo., 0 g fiber, 1 g pro. **Daily Values:** 4% vit. A, 99% vit. C, 1% calcium, 3% iron

*See note, page 116.

CHICKEN AND SHRIMP TORTILLA SOUP

Shrimp cook superfast (and get overcooked fast too), so add them just three minutes before you're ready to serve. If you want a little fire in your soup bowl, float thin rings of fresh jalapeño on top, or spike it with hot pepper sauce.

Start to Finish: 30 minutes   **Makes:** 6 servings (7¾ cups)

- 6 ounces fresh or frozen medium shrimp, peeled and deveined
- 1 recipe Crisp Tortilla Shreds
- 1 large onion, chopped
- 1 teaspoon cumin seeds
- 1 tablespoon cooking oil
- 4½ cups reduced-sodium chicken broth
- 1 14½-ounce can Mexican-style stewed tomatoes, undrained
- 3 tablespoons snipped fresh cilantro
- 2 tablespoons lime juice
- 1⅔ cups shredded cooked chicken breast

1 Thaw shrimp, if frozen. Prepare Crisp Tortilla Shreds; set aside.

2 In a large saucepan cook the onion and cumin seeds in hot oil about 5 minutes or until onion is tender. Carefully add chicken broth, undrained tomatoes, cilantro, and lime juice.

3 Bring to boiling; reduce heat. Simmer, covered, for 8 minutes. Stir in shrimp and chicken. Cook about 3 minutes more or until shrimp turn pink, stirring occasionally. Top each serving with tortilla shreds.

143

Crisp Tortilla Shreds: Brush four 5½-inch corn tortillas with 1 tablespoon cooking oil. In a small bowl combine ½ teaspoon salt and ⅛ teaspoon ground black pepper; sprinkle mixture on tortillas. Cut tortillas into thin strips. Arrange in a single layer on a baking sheet. Bake in a 350°F oven about 8 minutes or until crisp.

Nutrition Facts per serving: 240 cal., 7 g total fat (1 g sat. fat), 76 mg chol., 1,356 mg sodium, 21 g carbo., 1 g fiber, 23 g pro. **Daily Values:** 3% vit. A, 28% vit. C, 6% calcium, 16% iron

BOLILLOS

When you make these crusty rolls, your house will fill with the heady aroma of a *panaderia* (Mexican bakery). Serve them with dinner or, for a bread-and-chocolate breakfast, enjoy them in the morning with a cup of Cinnamon Hot Chocolate (see recipe, page 139).

Prep: 45 minutes   **Rise:** 1 hour 30 minutes   **Bake:** 25 minutes   **Oven:** 375°F   **Makes:** 12 rolls

3¾ to 4¼ cups all-purpose flour
1 package active dry yeast
1 tablespoon sugar
¾ teaspoon salt

1½ cups warm water (120°F to 130°F)
   Cornmeal
1 egg white
1 tablespoon milk or water

1 In a large mixing bowl combine 1½ cups of the flour, the yeast, sugar, and salt; add warm water. Beat with an electric mixer on low to medium speed for 30 seconds, scraping sides of bowl. Beat on high speed for 3 minutes. Using a wooden spoon, stir in as much of the remaining flour as you can.

2 Turn dough out onto a lightly floured surface. Knead in enough of the remaining flour to make a moderately stiff dough that is smooth and elastic (knead 6 to 8 minutes total). Shape dough into a ball. Place in a lightly greased bowl, turning once to grease surface of dough. Cover and let rise in a warm place until doubled in size (about 1 hour).

3 Punch dough down. Turn dough out onto a lightly floured surface. Divide dough into 12 portions. Shape each portion into an oval about 5 inches long. Pull and twist ends slightly.

4 Sprinkle cornmeal over 2 lightly greased baking sheets. Transfer rolls to baking sheets. Use a sharp knife to make a cut about ¼ inch deep along center of each roll.

5 In a small bowl combine egg white and milk. Brush some of the egg white mixture over the tops and sides of rolls. Cover and let rise until nearly doubled in size (30 to 45 minutes).

6 Bake in a 375° oven for 15 minutes. Brush again with some of the egg white mixture. Bake about 10 minutes more or until golden brown. Remove rolls from baking sheets. Cool on wire racks.

Make-ahead tip: Prepare and bake rolls as directed. Cool completely. Place baked rolls in a freezer container or resealable bag and freeze for up to 3 months. Before serving, thaw rolls at room temperature.

Nutrition Facts per roll: 141 cal., 1 g total fat, (0 g sat. fat), 1 mg chol., 152 mg sodium, 29 g carbo., 1 g fiber, 4 g pro.
Daily Values: 1% calcium, 10% iron

BREAD PUDDING

This recipe calls for a plantain, also called the "cooking banana" because it's really only good when baked, fried, or boiled. Thicker skinned and less sweet than its more familiar cousin, the banana, the plantain is best used when bright yellow with a few black speckles. A medium plantain weighs about 8 ounces.

Prep: 25 minutes   **Bake:** 35 minutes   **Oven:** 350°F   **Makes:** 6 to 8 servings

2 Bolillos* (see recipe, page 144)
¾ cup water
½ cup packed brown sugar
3 inches stick cinnamon
2 whole cloves
2 apples, peeled, cored, and sliced
1 ripe medium plantain or large firm banana, sliced

⅓ cup raisins
¼ cup coarsely chopped almonds, toasted
½ cup shredded asadero, Chihuahua, or Monterey Jack cheese (optional)
1 recipe Crema Espesa (optional)

1 To dry bread, tear bolillos into small pieces to equal about 2 cups. Place bread pieces on a baking sheet. Bake in a 350° oven for 8 to 10 minutes or until dried.

2 Meanwhile, for syrup, in a small saucepan combine water, brown sugar, stick cinnamon, and cloves. Bring to boiling; reduce heat. Boil gently, uncovered, for 8 to 10 minutes or until reduced to ¾ cup. Remove the spices with a slotted spoon; discard the spices.

3 In a large bowl toss together dried bread pieces and syrup. Add sliced apples, plantain slices, raisins, and almonds; toss gently. Transfer mixture to an ungreased 2-quart square baking dish.

4 Bake, covered, in a 350° oven for 35 to 40 minutes or until apples are tender. Remove from oven. If desired, sprinkle with cheese and serve with Crema Espesa. Serve warm.

*Note: French bread may be substituted for the bolillos. Choose firm-textured bread for best results.

Nutrition Facts per serving: 235 cal., 3 g total fat (.3 g sat. fat), 0 mg chol., 61 mg sodium, 51 g carbo., 3 g fiber, 3 g pro.
Daily Values: 6% vit. A, 12% vit. C, 4% calcium, 9% iron

Crema Espesa: In a small saucepan heat 1 cup whipping cream (not ultrapasteurized) over low heat until warm (90°F to 100°F). Pour the cream into a small bowl. Stir in 2 tablespoons buttermilk. Cover and let mixture stand at room temperature for 24 to 30 hours (do not stir) or until mixture is thickened. Store in a covered container in the refrigerator for up to 1 week. Stir before serving. Makes 1 cup.

MEXICAN RICE

Mexican rice may be similar to Spanish rice, but they differ in one significant way: The color of Spanish rice traditionally is bright yellow, thanks to the addition of saffron. Mexican rice, a simple combination of rice, broth, and vegetables, is a great complement to refried beans (see recipe, page 124).

Prep: 15 minutes   **Cook:** 25 minutes   **Stand:** 10 minutes   **Makes:** 6 cups (twelve ½-cup servings)

1 cup chopped unpeeled roma tomatoes

½ cup chopped onion

1 to 2 cloves garlic

½ cup cooking oil

1½ cups uncooked long grain white rice

3½ cups warm chicken broth

½ cup fresh or frozen peas or chopped zucchini

½ cup chopped carrots

1 Combine tomatoes, onion, and garlic in a blender container or food processor bowl. Cover and blend or process until smooth.

2 Heat oil in a large saucepan over medium heat. Carefully add rice. Cook and stir for 8 to 10 minutes or until rice is golden in color. Drain any excess oil. Stir in tomato puree. Cook and stir for 4 to 6 minutes or until puree is absorbed.

3 Add broth and peas and carrots. Bring to boiling over medium-high heat; reduce heat and simmer, uncovered, over medium heat for 12 to 15 minutes or until liquid is nearly absorbed. Cover. Remove from heat and let stand about 10 minutes before serving to let rice steam and absorb remaining liquid. Fluff rice with fork before serving.

Nutrition Facts per ½-cup serving: 136 cal., 4 g total fat (0 g sat. fat), 0 mg chol., 231 mg sodium, 21 g carbo., 1 g fiber, 4 g pro. **Daily Values:** 10% vit. C, 1% calcium, 7% iron

CORN TORTILLAS

Corn tortillas, the staff of life of modern Mexico, have been popular since pre-Columbian times. Purchased tortillas simply don't compare to fresh. To make your own, all you need is corn tortilla flour, or *masa harina* (literally "dough flour," made from dried corn kernels cooked in lime water), water, and two nimble hands.

Prep: 20 minutes   **Cook:** 2 minutes per tortilla   **Stand:** 15 minutes   **Makes:** twelve 6-inch tortillas

2 cups instant corn tortilla flour   **1¼ cups warm water**

1 In a medium bowl combine tortilla flour and water. Stir mixture together until dough is firm but moist (if necessary, add more water, 1 tablespoon at a time). Let dough rest for 15 minutes.

2 Divide the dough into 12 portions; shape each portion into a ball. Using a tortilla press or rolling pin, flatten each ball between 2 pieces of waxed paper into a 6-inch circle.

3 Carefully peel off top sheet of waxed paper. Place tortilla, paper side up, on a medium-hot ungreased griddle or skillet. As tortilla begins to heat, carefully peel off remaining sheet of waxed paper (this should take about 20 seconds). Cook, turning occasionally, for 2 to 2½ minutes or until tortilla is dry and light brown. Wrap tortillas in foil if using immediately.

Make-ahead tip: To freeze tortillas, stack them, alternating each tortilla with 2 layers of waxed paper. Wrap the stack in a moisture- and vapor-proof bag, foil, or freezer wrap. Seal tightly and freeze for up to 1 month. Thaw completely before using.

Nutrition Facts per tortilla: 73 cal., 1 g total fat (0 g sat. fat), 0 mg chol., 2 mg sodium, 15 g carbo., 1 g fiber, 2 g pro.
Daily Values: 4% calcium, 3% iron

A tortilla press speeds things along. Note that the dough is placed off-center toward the hinge of the press.

Apply firm, even pressure to the handle. Lining the press with waxed paper allows you to move tortillas easily without breaking.

TURKEY WITH MOLE

Mistaking mole (MO-lay) sauce for chocolate sauce is a common misconception. More accurately, mole means "concoction" in Spanish. In addition to a little chocolate, it is flavored with chiles, sesame or pumpkin seeds, spices, and nuts.

Prep: 1½ hours   **Bake:** 1½ hours   **Oven:** 350°F   **Makes:** 8 to 10 servings

3 dried ancho chile peppers**	½ teaspoon ground cinnamon
2 dried pasilla chile peppers	¼ teaspoon coriander seeds, toasted*
2 dried mulato chile peppers	¼ teaspoon anise seeds, toasted*
3 cups hot chicken broth	⅛ teaspoon ground black pepper
1 7½-ounce can whole tomatoes, undrained	Dash ground cloves
½ cup chopped onion	1 tablespoon lard or vegetable oil
⅓ cup blanched whole almonds, toasted*	1 tablespoon sugar
¼ cup raisins	1 teaspoon salt
1 6-inch corn tortilla, toasted* and torn	2 tablespoons lard or vegetable oil
2 tablespoons sesame seeds, toasted*	1 8- to 10-pound turkey, cut up
1 ounce unsweetened chocolate, chopped	Sesame seeds, toasted (optional)*
1 clove garlic	

150

1 For mole, in a dry skillet over medium heat toast dry peppers, turning occasionally until they have a toasted aroma, about 8 minutes. Let cool. Wearing disposable plastic gloves or small plastic bags, remove stems, seeds, and ribs from peppers.** Tear peppers into pieces and place in a bowl. Cover with hot broth and soak for 30 minutes to soften. Strain soaking liquid through 100-percent-cotton cheesecloth; reserve soaking liquid (you should have about 2½ cups.).

2 In a large bowl combine drained peppers, undrained tomatoes, onion, almonds, raisins, torn tortilla, sesame seeds, chocolate, garlic, cinnamon, coriander seeds, anise seeds, black pepper, and cloves. In a blender container or food processor bowl process or blend the pepper mixture, half at a time, to make a coarse puree.

3 In a medium saucepan heat 1 tablespoon lard over medium heat. Add mole puree; cook about 5 minutes or until darkened and thick, stirring often. Slowly stir in 1¼ cups of the reserved soaking liquid. Cook and stir over medium-low heat for 5 minutes or until mixture is the consistency of heavy cream. Stir in sugar and salt. Set aside.

4 In an extra-large skillet heat 2 tablespoons lard over medium-high heat. Brown turkey pieces, about half at a time, for 3 to 4 minutes per side. Place in a roasting pan. Coat all surfaces of the turkey pieces with 2 cups of the mole.

5 Bake, covered, in a 350° oven for 1½ to 2 hours or until turkey is tender, no longer pink inside, and a thermometer inserted into breast registers 170°F and registers 180°F in drumsticks and thighs. Reheat remaining mole and serve with turkey. If desired, sprinkle with sesame seeds.

*Note: Toast almonds, tortilla, spices, and almonds individually in a dry skillet over medium heat for 1 to 3 minutes, stirring or turning frequently. Watch spices carefully so they do not burn. It's best to toast these ingredients while the peppers soften.

Nutrition Facts per serving: 482 cal., 26 g total fat (8 g sat. fat), 121 mg chol., 729 mg sodium, 18 g carbo., 4 g fiber, 45 g pro. **Daily Values:** 11% vit. C, 9% calcium, 28% iron

**See note, page 116.

MEXICAN SHORTBREAD COOKIES

Cinnamon and almonds—two of Mexico's favorite flavors—give these basic shortbread cookies a Latino touch. The almond is a symbol of happiness. Maybe that's how these cookies came to be known as Mexican wedding cakes.

Prep: 30 minutes   **Bake:** 20 minutes per batch   **Oven:** 325°F   **Makes:** 48 cookies

1   cup butter
½   cup sifted powdered sugar
1   tablespoon water
1   teaspoon vanilla
2   cups all-purpose flour

½   cup ground almonds, toasted
¼   teaspoon ground cinnamon or
    2 teaspoons finely shredded
    orange peel
¾   to 1 cup sifted powdered sugar

1 In a medium mixing bowl beat butter with an electric mixer on medium to high speed for 30 seconds. Add the ½ cup powdered sugar and beat until fluffy. Beat in the water and vanilla until combined. Beat in as much of the flour as you can with the mixer. Stir in any remaining flour, almonds, and cinnamon. If necessary, chill the dough for 1 hour or until easy to handle.

2 Shape dough into 1-inch balls. Place on an ungreased baking sheet.

152

3 Bake in a 325° oven about 20 minutes or until bottoms are light brown. Cool cookies on a wire rack. Gently shake cooled cookies, a few at a time, in a plastic bag with the ¾ to 1 cup powdered sugar.

Nutrition Facts per cookie: 67 cal., 5 g total fat (2 g sat. fat), 11 mg chol., 41 mg sodium, 7 g carbo., 0 g fiber, 1 g pro.
Daily Values: 3% vit. A, 1% calcium, 2% iron

¡Menu

Chayote salad

Chilled avocado soup

Mango salsa

Chicken with new mexican-style Rub

CHAYOTE SALAD

The chayote, a relative of zucchini, looks like a very large pear and has a crisp, firm texture and moist flesh that tastes something like a cucumber and an apple. A good source of potassium, it is widely available during the winter months.

Prep: 30 minutes   **Marinate:** 3 hours   **Makes:** 6 side-dish servings

- 3 medium chayotes, peeled, seeded, and coarsely chopped
- 1 cup canned garbanzo beans, rinsed and drained
- ¼ cup lemon juice
- ¼ cup olive oil or salad oil
- ¼ cup water
- 1 tablespoon snipped fresh basil or 1 teaspoon dried basil, crushed
- ½ teaspoon sugar
- ¼ teaspoon salt
- 2 cloves garlic, minced
- ¼ cup sliced pitted ripe olives
- 6 lettuce leaves
- 2 medium tomatoes, cut into wedges
  Thinly sliced red onion

1 In a medium saucepan cook chayotes, covered, in a small amount of boiling salted water for 5 to 6 minutes or until tender; drain. Rinse with cold water to stop cooking; drain well. Transfer to a medium bowl; add garbanzo beans.

2 For marinade, in a screw-top jar combine lemon juice, olive oil, water, basil, sugar, salt, and garlic. Cover and shake well. Pour marinade over chayote mixture, stirring to coat well. Cover and marinate in the refrigerator for 3 to 24 hours, stirring occasionally.

3 To serve, drain chayote mixture, reserving marinade. Stir in olives. Spoon chayote mixture onto 6 lettuce-lined plates. Top servings with tomato wedges and red onion. Drizzle with some of the reserved marinade.

Nutrition Facts per serving: 170 cal., 10 g total fat (1 g sat. fat), 0 mg chol., 273 mg sodium, 18 g carbo., 4 g fiber, 3 g pro. **Daily Values:** 9% vit. A, 39% vit. C, 4% calcium, 8% iron

CHILLED AVOCADO SOUP

You can make this creamy appetizer up to a day ahead of serving. Perfectly ripe avocados are firm but yield to gentle pressure. To ripen avocados, place them in a brown paper bag and set them on the countertop for 2 to 4 days. Store ripe avocados in the refrigerator for a few days to keep them at their prime.

Prep: 15 minutes   **Chill:** 3 hours   **Makes:** 6 side-dish servings

3 ripe avocados, halved, seeded, and peeled (1¼ pounds)

1 cup chicken broth

¼ cup water

1 cup half-and-half or light cream

¼ teaspoon salt

⅛ teaspoon onion powder

Dash ground white pepper

1 tablespoon lemon juice

Lemon slices (optional)

1 Place avocados in a blender container or food processor bowl. Add chicken broth and water; cover and blend or process until smooth. Add half-and-half, salt, onion powder, and white pepper. Cover and blend or process until combined. Transfer to a large bowl. Stir in lemon juice. Cover and refrigerate at least 3 hours or up to 24 hours. Stir before serving. If desired, garnish with lemon slices.

Nutrition Facts per serving: 167 cal., 15 g total fat (5 g sat. fat), 15 mg chol., 287 mg sodium, 7 g carbo., 3 g fiber, 3 g pro.
Daily Values: 12% vit. A, 11% vit. C, 5% calcium, 4% iron

MANGO SALSA

This tropical fruit salsa is especially good served over grilled fish or pork.

Prep: 20 minutes   **Chill:** 2 hours   **Makes:** about 2 cups (eight ¼-cup servings)

1½ cups chopped, peeled mango, papaya,
    peaches, plums, and/or pineapple

½ cup chopped red or green sweet pepper

¼ cup thinly sliced green onions

¼ cup snipped fresh cilantro or parsley

2 tablespoons lime juice or lemon juice

1 to 2 fresh jalapeño or serrano
   peppers, seeded and finely chopped,
   or 2 tablespoons finely chopped fresh
   Anaheim pepper*

1 In a medium bowl stir together fruit, sweet pepper, green onions, cilantro, lime juice, and jalapeño. Cover; chill at least 2 hours before serving.

Nutrition Facts per serving: 26 cal., 0 g total fat (0 g sat. fat), 0 mg chol., 3 mg sodium, 6 g carbo., 1 g fiber, 0 g pro.
Daily Values: 37% vit. A, 52% vit. C, 1% calcium, 1% iron

*See note, page 116.

CHICKEN WITH NEW MEXICAN-STYLE RUB

In traditional Mexico, this aromatic rub is made in the chiseled-out bowls of basalt, or lava rock, called "molcajetes" that are found in nearly every kitchen. In America, you're more likely to use a mortar and pestle, which does the same job just as well. Keep the additional rub around for quick-to-fix weeknight meals.

Prep: 15 minutes   **Broil:** 12 minutes   **Makes:** 4 servings

1 tablespoon dried oregano

1 tablespoon dried thyme

1 teaspoon coriander seeds

1 teaspoon anise seeds

¼ cup chili powder

1 teaspoon paprika

½ teaspoon cracked black pepper

¼ teaspoon salt

4 skinless, boneless chicken breast halves (about 1¼ pounds total)

1 For rub, using a mortar and pestle, grind together the oregano, thyme, coriander seeds, and anise seeds. Stir in chili powder, paprika, black pepper, and salt. Set seasoning mixture aside.*

2 With your fingers, gently rub some of the seasoning mixture onto both sides of the chicken breast halves.

3 Place chicken on the unheated rack of a broiler pan. Broil 4 to 5 inches from heat for 12 to 15 minutes or until tender and no longer pink, turning once. (Or grill on the rack of an uncovered grill directly over medium coals for 12 to 15 minutes or until tender and no longer pink, turning once.)

*Note: The seasoning rub makes about 7 tablespoons. Store the leftover mixture, covered, in a cool, dry place and use within 6 months.

Nutrition Facts per serving: 207 cal., 4 g total fat (1 g sat. fat), 82 mg chol., 299 mg sodium, 6 g carbo., 3 g fiber, 34 g pro.
Daily Values: 66% vit. A, 11% vit. C, 8% calcium, 21% iron

158

BUÑUELOS

Serve these thin deep-fried pastries while they're still warm with a cup of full-bodied coffee. They're unforgettable drizzled with caramel syrup or dusted with cinnamon sugar.

Prep: 1 hour   **Cook:** 2 minutes per batch   **Oven:** 300°F   **Makes:** 24 buñuelos

2 cups all-purpose flour
1 teaspoon baking powder
½ teaspoon salt
¼ teaspoon cream of tartar
2 tablespoons shortening

2 beaten eggs
⅓ cup milk
   Cooking oil for frying
1 recipe Brown Sugar Syrup or Cinnamon Sugar

1 In a large bowl combine flour, baking powder, salt, and cream of tartar. Cut in shortening until mixture resembles coarse crumbs. Make a well in the center of the flour mixture.

2 In a small bowl combine eggs and milk. Add to flour mixture all at once. Stir just until dough clings together.

3 Turn dough out onto a lightly floured surface; knead dough about 2 minutes or until soft and smooth. Divide dough into 24 portions. Shape each portion into a ball. Cover dough and let rest for 15 minutes.

4 In a heavy 10-inch skillet heat about ¾ inch of cooking oil to 375°F. Meanwhile, on a lightly floured surface roll each ball to a 4-inch circle. Fry dough circles in hot oil about 1 minute on each side or until golden brown. Drain on paper towels. Keep warm in a 300° oven while frying remaining dough. Drizzle with Brown Sugar Syrup.

Brown Sugar Syrup: In a small saucepan combine 1 cup packed dark brown sugar and ½ cup water. Cook and stir over medium-high heat until sugar is dissolved. Add a 3-inch stick cinnamon or a dash of ground cinnamon. Bring to boiling; reduce heat. Simmer, uncovered, for 5 minutes. Remove from heat. Stir in ½ teaspoon vanilla. Discard cinnamon stick. Serve warm. Makes about ¾ cup syrup.

Cinnamon Sugar: Stir together ½ cup granulated sugar and 1 teaspoon ground cinnamon. Sprinkle over warm buñuelos.

Nutrition Facts per buñuelo: 170 cal., 10 g total fat (2 g sat. fat), 18 mg chol., 76 mg sodium, 17 g carbo., 0 g fiber, 2 g pro. **Daily Values:** 1% vit. A, 3% calcium, 4% iron

Indian

161

Though other cuisines are better known to Americans, those who are introduced to Indian food almost always become passionate about it. And why wouldn't they, with its myriad spices to roast, grind, and blend in new ways and its flatbreads to nibble.

Indians did not have a strong presence in America until the turn of the 20th century, when a great drought hit the Punjabi region and about 7,000 Indians came to this country. Between 1923 and 1965, America tightened its immigration belt and few Indians gained entrance. But in the late 1960s, when laws loosened up, there was once again an influx of Indian immigrants, this one much larger. That wave of immigration, which happened to coincide with the 1968 visit by the Beatles to India on a spiritual pilgrimage, piqued the interest of Americans.

College students and the generally adventuresome began wearing brightly colored silks, Madras prints, and Nehru jackets. They also swayed to ragas played by sitar master Ravi Shankar. The interest in Indian culture naturally led the curious into the kitchen, where they began to learn how to make aromatic curries, tandoori chicken, and sweet-and-sour chutneys.

No longer foreign to these lands, Indian food adds spice to everyday American culture at large. As recently as the 1990s, many Americans began trading their bitter morning brew for sweet and aromatic chai. And who knows what other culinary treats lie ahead? Considering India's great size and diverse peoples, America is only beginning to discover its glorious foods.

cilantro

basmati rice

garam masala

cardamom pods and

cumin seeds

Exotic and mysterious, Indian ingredients are among the most enticing in the world for many cooks. Of the myriad enchanting ingredients from this large and populous country, it may be the spices and rice that hold the most allure. Here are a few spices to consider, along with a major variety of rice.

The plant from which **cardamom** is harvested is actually a member of the ginger family, native to southern India and Sri Lanka. Cardamom has been enjoyed for at least a thousand years, and in addition to being crucial to Indian cuisine, it has become important in Scandinavian cooking. Cooks are sometimes confused about how to use cardamom, as it is sold in several different forms including powder, seeds, and whole pods containing the seeds. Seeds and whole pods generally impart more flavor than powder because cardamom's flavorful oils break down more rapidly once the seeds have been crushed.

The term **curry** can be applied to a spicy Indian dish, a type of leaf used in several types of Indian dishes, and a blend of aromatic spices—curry powder. A blend of many spices (up to 20), curry powder varies widely in flavor and spicy heat level from region to region. Among the most common components of curry powder are coriander, cumin, mustard seeds, red and black pepper, fenugreek, turmeric, and, at times, cinnamon, cloves, and cardamom. Although one might guess that curry leaf would be included in curry powder, it's not.

Garam masala is a spice blend from northern India known for its heat. Like curry powder, specific blends vary widely, but popular ingredients include cinnamon, cloves, black pepper, cardamom, coriander, and cumin.

Of the world's rices, **basmati** is one of the most prized, particularly for its distinctive flavor and aroma. Basmati is a long grain rice that is very slender and often quite low in starch, making it one of the least sticky varieties. When basmati rice is carefully rinsed before cooking to remove its surface starch, it becomes exceptionally fluffy when cooked, with a light, delicate texture. Basmati rice is an almost essential complement to many Indian dishes.

Menu

Potatoes
with Yogurt Sauce

Spicy Oven-Baked
Chicken

Naan Bread

Cilantro Chutney

Mithai*

*Mithai is a name for various Indian sweets.
(See glossary, page 276.) Purchase them at
Indian markets or see resources, page 279.

POTATOES WITH YOGURT SAUCE

This dish, like many Indian dishes, is best when you toast the spices prior to combining them with the main ingredients. The result, in this case, is a warm, intensified mix of cumin and cayenne.

Prep: 20 minutes   **Cook:** 15 minutes   **Makes:** 4 to 6 servings

1½ **pounds round red or white potatoes, peeled and cut into 1-inch pieces**

⅔ **cup plain yogurt**

1 **teaspoon salt**

¼ **teaspoon freshly ground black pepper**

2 **tablespoons cooking oil**

1½ **teaspoons cumin seeds, crushed**

   Dash cayenne pepper

2 **tablespoons finely chopped fresh cilantro**

1 In a large saucepan cook potatoes, covered, in enough boiling water to cover for 12 to 15 minutes or just until potatoes are tender. Drain potatoes in a colander; set aside.

2 Whisk together yogurt, salt, and black pepper; set aside. Heat oil in the same large saucepan. Add cumin seeds and cayenne. Gently stir in potatoes. Cook and stir for 4 minutes. Remove from heat; gently stir in yogurt mixture and cilantro. Transfer to serving bowl. Serve warm or at room temperature.

Nutrition Facts per serving: 190 cal., 7 g total fat (1 g sat. fat), 2 mg chol., 619 mg sodium, 26 g carbo., 2 g fiber, 5 g pro.
Daily Values: 3% vit. A, 35% vit. C, 9% calcium, 9% iron

SPICY OVEN-BAKED CHICKEN

A paste of lemon juice and spices rubbed under the skin of the chicken in this Indian-inspired dish infuses the meat with flavor even before it's roasted to crisp and aromatic perfection.

Prep: 25 minutes   **Bake:** 40 to 45 minutes   **Chill:** 2 hours   **Oven:** 400°F   **Makes:** 4 servings

2 tablespoons fresh lemon juice	½ teaspoon ground garam masala
2 teaspoons ground turmeric	¼ teaspoon ground allspice
1½ teaspoons paprika	¼ teaspoon cayenne pepper
1 clove garlic, minced	2¼ pounds meaty chicken pieces
½ teaspoon salt	2 teaspoons cooking oil

1 In a small bowl combine lemon juice, 1½ teaspoons of the turmeric, the paprika, garlic, salt, garam masala, allspice, and cayenne.

2 Loosen chicken skin slightly and rub spice mixture under skin. Place drumsticks and thighs (skin `side up) in a shallow roasting pan. Combine remaining turmeric and oil; brush on chicken. Cover and chill for 2 to 4 hours.

3 Bake, uncovered, in a 400° oven for 40 to 45 minutes or until a meat thermometer inserted into thickest portion registers 180°F.

Nutrition Facts per serving: 367 cal., 23 g total fat (6 g sat. fat), 151 mg chol., 410 mg sodium, 2 g carbo., 0 g fiber, 34 g pro. **Daily Values:** 15% vit. A, 14% vit. C, 3% calcium, 15% iron

NAAN BREAD

Despite the fact that it's a leavened bread, naan is still supposed to be relatively flat. To keep it from rising and puffing too much, roll only as many balls of dough as will fit on your baking stone. While one batch is baking, you can roll out the next, and so on.

Prep: 30 minutes   **Rise:** 1 hour   **Bake:** 3 minutes   **Stand:** 25 minutes   **Oven:** 475°F
Makes: 8 naan rounds

⅓ **cup warm milk (100°F to 110°F)**
2 **teaspoons sugar**
1 **package active dry yeast**
½ **cup plain yogurt**
3 **tablespoons purchased ghee* or clarified butter****

1 **teaspoon salt**
1 **teaspoon baking powder**
2 **cups all-purpose flour**

1 In a medium bowl combine milk, sugar, and yeast. Let stand for 5 minutes or until foamy. Add yogurt, ghee, salt, and baking powder. Add flour and stir until mixture forms a ball.

2 Turn dough out onto a lightly floured surface. Knead for 4 to 5 minutes or until dough is smooth. Place dough in a greased bowl, turning to coat. Cover and let rise for 1 hour or until dough is doubled in size.

3 Determine how many 6-inch rounds will fit on your baking stone at one time. Place baking stone on the lowest rack in the oven. Preheat oven to 475°. Divide dough into 8 pieces; shape into balls. Cover balls with plastic wrap and let stand for 20 minutes.

4 On a lightly floured surface, roll enough balls of dough to fit onto baking stone into 6-inch circles. Place dough circles on hot baking stone. Bake for 2 to 3 minutes or until brown. Turn circles over. Bake for 1 to 2 minutes more or until brown and slightly puffed. Remove naan from oven and wrap in foil to keep warm. Repeat with remaining dough. Serve hot.

*Note: Ghee is an Indian version of clarified butter which is available in specialty markets.

**Clarified Butter: Melt ¼ cup butter over very low heat without stirring; cool slightly. Pour off and reserve clear top layer; discard milky bottom layer.

Nutrition Facts per round: 172 cal., 6 g total fat, (0 g sat. fat), 1 mg chol., 359 mg sodium, 25 g carbo., 1 g fiber, 4 g pro. **Daily Values:** 1% vit. A, 1% vit. C, 8% calcium, 9% iron

171

CILANTRO CHUTNEY

An Indian meal is never complete without some kind of relish. A relish may be as simple as a single green chile or as complex as lime pickle, which requires a multitude of ingredients and years to mature. Chutneys may be sweet, sour, sweet-and-sour, salty, savory, or hot. This one is just a little hot, with loads of fresh lime and cilantro flavor.

Start to Finish: 20 minutes   **Makes:** ½ cup (eight 1-tablespoon servings)

2	cups loosely packed fresh cilantro leaves	1	tablespoon fresh lime juice or lemon juice
½	cup chopped onion	1	teaspoon sugar
½	to 1 hot green chile (such as serrano), seeds and membranes removed*	¼	teaspoon salt
		¼	teaspoon ground cumin

1 Combine all ingredients in a food processor. Cover and process until chutney mixture is almost smooth. Serve at once or cover and serve within 2 hours.

Nutrition Facts per tablespoon: 12 cal., 0 g total fat, (0 g sat. fat), 0 mg chol., 81 mg sodium, 2 g carbo., 0 g pro.
Daily Values: 16% vit. A, 36% vit. C, 2% calcium, 5% iron

172

*Note: Because hot peppers, such as habañeros and other chiles, contain volatile oils that can burn your skin and eyes, avoid direct contact with them as much as possible. When working with chile peppers, wear plastic or rubber gloves. If your bare hands do touch the peppers, wash your hands well with soap and water.

MENU

Pooris

Garlic Chutney

Vegetable Curry

Spiced Basmati with
Peanuts

Fresh Spiced Fruit

POORIS (FRIED PUFFY BREAD)

As you fry the breads, one by one, keep the finished pooris warm on a paper towel-lined baking sheet or plate in a 300°F oven. Then, when the cooking is done, you can enjoy them while they're hot!

Prep: 30 minutes **Cook:** 1 minute each **Stand:** 30 minutes **Makes:** 12 pooris

⅔ **cup whole wheat flour**

⅔ **cup cake flour**

½ **cup all-purpose flour**

1 **teaspoon salt**

2 **tablespoons cooking oil**

½ **cup warm milk or water (100°F to 110°F)**

Cooking oil for frying

1 In a large bowl, combine whole wheat flour, cake flour, all-purpose flour, and salt. Add the 2 tablespoons oil; stir with a fork or rub with your fingers until mixture resembles coarse crumbs. Stir in milk until dough forms a ball. Turn dough out onto a lightly floured surface. Knead a few minutes to make a moderately stiff dough. Shape dough into a ball. Place in a lightly greased bowl, turning once to grease surface of dough. Cover; let rest for 30 minutes.

2 In a deep fryer or deep saucepan, heat 1½ inches of oil to 350°F. Meanwhile, divide dough into 12 pieces. Roll pieces into balls, then roll balls into 4- to 5-inch circles. Keep circles covered with plastic wrap until ready to fry.

3 Carefully add one dough circle to hot oil. When poori puffs, turn it over and fry until second side is golden (about 1 minute total). Remove poori from oil with tongs; drain on paper towels. Repeat until all pooris have been fried. Serve immediately.

Nutrition Facts per poori: 140 cal., 8 g total fat (1 g sat. fat), 1 mg chol., 199 mg sodium, 13 g carbo., 1 g fiber, 2 g pro.
Daily Values: 2% calcium, 5% iron

174

Pooris must be carefully added to hot oil to avoid splatters. Maintain a safe distance from the oil.

Pooris fry quickly in 350°F oil. Long-handled tongs are ideal for handling them safely and securely.

GARLIC CHUTNEY

You can use this sweet, spicy coconut chutney in many flavorful ways: It's wonderful stirred into pureed soups or stir-fries, eaten with naan or pooris, or served alongside grilled shrimp. It's also great with Vegetable Curry (see recipe, page 177).

Start to Finish: 5 minutes   **Makes:** 1 cup (sixteen 1-tablespoon servings)

1	cup unsweetened coconut	½	teaspoon salt
2	cloves garlic, halved	¼	teaspoon crushed red pepper
1	tablespoon lime juice	¾	cup water

1 Place coconut, garlic, lime juice, salt, red pepper, and water in a food processor bowl. Cover and process until almost smooth. Serve with vegetable curry.

Storage tip: Cover and chill for up to 1 week. If necessary, stir in additional water to thin.

Nutrition Facts per tablespoon: 22 cal., 1 g total fat (1 g sat. fat), 0 g chol., 85 mg sodium, 2 g carbo., 0 g fiber, 0 g pro. **Daily Values:** 1% vit. C, 1% iron

VEGETABLE CURRY

The phrase "garam masala" simply means "hot spices." This varied blend of up to 12 spices originates from the cold of northern India and may include cloves, cinnamon, bay leaf, black pepper, nutmeg, mace, and cardamom. Traditionally, it's believed to bring heat to the body.

Prep: 20 minutes   **Cook:** 15 minutes   **Makes:** 4 servings

- 2 tablespoons cooking oil
- 1 teaspoon cumin seeds, crushed
- 1 clove garlic, minced
- 1 teaspoon salt
- 1 teaspoon garam masala
- 1 teaspoon grated fresh ginger
- ½ teaspoon ground turmeric
- ¼ to ½ teaspoon cayenne pepper
- 2 medium tomatoes, seeded and chopped

- 2 medium potatoes, peeled and diced (about 1½ cups)
- ½ cup chopped carrot
- ½ cup frozen cut green beans
- ½ cup frozen peas
- 2 cups water
- ¼ cup raisins
- ¼ cup whipping cream (optional)
- 2 cups hot cooked basmati rice
- Fresh cilantro leaves

1 In a large skillet heat oil over medium heat. Add cumin seeds. Cook and stir for 10 seconds. Add garlic, salt, garam masala, ginger, turmeric, and cayenne. Cook and stir for 15 seconds (watch closely to avoid burning). Add tomatoes, potatoes, carrot, green beans, peas, water, and raisins. Bring to boiling; reduce heat. Simmer, covered, for 15 to 20 minutes or until vegetables are tender. If desired, stir in cream. Serve with rice. Garnish with cilantro.

Nutrition Facts per serving: 282 cal., 7 g total fat (1 g sat. fat), 0 g chol., 623 mg sodium, 49 g carbo., 4 g fiber, 5 g pro.
Daily Values: 90% vit. A, 49% vit. C, 5% calcium, 18% iron

SPICED BASMATI RICE WITH PEANUTS

The average Indian eats between one-half and two-thirds of a pound of rice a day. Because of its expense, just a fraction of that is basmati rice. Basmati is prized both for its history (it has been grown in the foothills of the Himalaya mountains for thousands of years) and its unique aroma and flavor (it's aged to decrease its moisture content, a process that results in a perfumed scent and nutlike flavor).

Prep: 15 minutes   **Cook:** 20 minutes   **Makes:** 6 servings

- 1 **cup uncooked basmati rice**
- 2 **tablespoons cooking oil**
- 1 **teaspoon cumin seeds, crushed**
- ½ **cup chopped onion**
- ⅓ **cup unsalted dry-roasted peanuts**
- 1 **hot green chile (such as serrano), seeded and finely chopped***

- 1 **clove garlic, minced**
- 1 **teaspoon garam masala**
- ¼ **teaspoon salt**
- 2 **cups vegetable or chicken broth**

1 Place rice in a fine-mesh sieve. Run cool water over the rice for several minutes; drain well.

2 Heat oil in 2-quart saucepan. Add cumin seeds. Cook and stir for 10 seconds. Add onion, peanuts, chile, and garlic. Cook and stir for 4 to 5 minutes or until onion is tender. Add rice, garam masala, and salt. Cook and stir for 2 minutes. Add broth. Bring to boiling; reduce heat. Simmer, covered, for 15 to 20 minutes or until liquid is absorbed and rice is tender. Fluff rice before serving.

Nutrition Facts per serving: 223 cal., 9 g total fat (1 g sat. fat), 0 g chol., 432 mg sodium, 30 g carbo., 1 g fiber, 5 g pro.
Daily Values: 2% vit. A, 2% vit. C, 1% calcium, 11% iron

*See note, page 172.

Excess starch causes rice to become sticky. Careful rinsing beforehand helps ensure fluffy cooked rice.

Basmati rice is naturally lower in sticky starch than other varieties, so after surface rinsing, it yields an extraordinarily light texture.

FRESH SPICED FRUIT

Served as is, this is a refreshing salad. Topped with a little yogurt (or yogurt cheese) and honey, it's a lovely dessert.

Prep: 20 minutes   **Chill:** 1 hour   **Makes:** 4 servings

1 cup seeded watermelon chunks

1 cup seeded peeled papaya chunks

1 cup pineapple chunks

1 cup peeled mango chunks

2 tablespoons lime juice

$\frac{1}{8}$ to $\frac{1}{4}$ teaspoon freshly ground black pepper

$\frac{1}{8}$ teaspoon ground cardamom

1 Combine all ingredients in a serving bowl. Cover and chill at least 1 hour or up to 24 hours.

Nutrition Facts per serving: 82 cal., 0 g fat, (0 g sat. fat), 0 g chol., 5 mg sodium, 20 g carbo., 2 g fiber, 0 g pro.
Daily Values: 37% vit. A, 76% vit. C, 2% calcium, 2% iron

MENU

Aloo Ghobi • Papadums*

Curried Lentils & Vegetables

Sautéed Cabbage w/Carrots

Fish in Mustard Sauce

Peas & Carrots w/Cumin

Kulfi (Saffron-Pistachio)
Ice Cream

*Papadums a popular crispy flatbread.
(See Glossary, page 277.) Purchase them,
unbaked, at an Indian market or see
Resources, page 279.

ALOO GHOBI

The multiplicity of flavors in the curry powder and garam masala (both highly aromatic blends of spices) truly shines through in this vegetable stew.

Start to Finish: 30 minutes   **Makes:** 6 servings

1   large red onion, halved lengthwise and thinly sliced

1   tablespoon olive oil

2   teaspoons curry powder

1   teaspoon ground cumin

¼   teaspoon garam masala

⅛   teaspoon ground red pepper

3   cups medium cauliflower florets

1   14½-ounce can diced tomatoes, undrained

2   medium potatoes, peeled and cut into 1-inch cubes (1½ cups)

2   medium sweet potatoes, peeled and cut into 1-inch cubes (1½ cups)

1½ cups vegetable broth or water

¼   teaspoon salt

¼   teaspoon freshly ground black pepper

1   cup frozen peas

4½ cups hot cooked brown rice or couscous

1 In a large saucepan cook onion in hot oil over medium heat about 5 minutes or until tender. Add curry powder, cumin, garam masala, and red pepper. Cook and stir for 1 minute.

2 Stir in cauliflower, undrained tomatoes, potatoes, sweet potatoes, broth, salt, and black pepper. Bring to boiling; reduce heat. Simmer, covered, for 10 to 12 minutes or until potatoes are tender. Stir in peas; heat through. Serve the stew over brown rice.

Nutrition Facts per serving: 334 cal., 4 g total fat (1 g sat. fat), 0 mg chol., 510 mg sodium, 66 g carbo., 9 g fiber, 9 g pro.
Daily Values: 224% vit. A, 84% vit. C, 9% calcium, 13% iron

CURRIED LENTILS AND VEGETABLES

This is a classic *dal,* perhaps the most commonly eaten dish in India. Dal is a creamy melange of dried legumes, garlic, and spices. Serve it as a side dish with curry or roasted meats, or as a main dish with warm naan (see recipe, page 171) for scooping.

Prep: 15 minutes   **Cook:** 20 minutes   **Makes:** 4 servings

3 cups water	¼ teaspoon ground ginger
1½ cups lentils, rinsed and drained	1 clove garlic, minced
1 cup chopped carrots	½ teaspoon salt
1 cup chopped onion	1 cup plain low-fat yogurt
⅔ cup chopped celery	1 cup chopped tomato
4 teaspoons curry powder	2 tablespoons snipped fresh parsley or cilantro
1 teaspoon grated fresh ginger	

1 In a large saucepan combine water, lentils, carrot, onion, celery, curry powder, ginger, garlic, and salt. Bring to boiling; reduce heat. Simmer, covered, for 20 to 25 minutes or until lentils are tender and liquid is absorbed.

2 In a small bowl stir together yogurt, tomato, and parsley. Serve with the lentil mixture.

183

Nutrition Facts per serving: 332 cal., 2 g total fat (1 g sat. fat), 4 mg chol., 382 mg sodium, 57 g carbo., 25 g fiber, 25 g pro. **Daily Values:** 163% vit. A, 35% vit. C, 19% calcium, 38% iron

SAUTEED CABBAGE WITH CARROTS

The easiest way to shred cabbage for this dish is to cut a head of cabbage into wedges. Trim the core from each wedge, rub the wedges over the coarse side of a box grater, and watch your knuckles!

Start to Finish: 30 minutes   **Makes:** 4 servings

3 **tablespoons cooking oil**

1 **tablespoon brown mustard seeds, crushed**

¼ **teaspoon asafetida***

8 **cups shredded cabbage**

1 **cup shredded carrots**

½ **cup dried unsweetened coconut flakes**

¼ **cup finely chopped fresh cilantro**

1 **to 2 hot green chiles (such as serrano), seeded and cut into thin strips****

2 **tablespoons sugar**

1 **teaspoon salt**

1 **tablespoon lime juice**

⅓ **cup chopped unsalted dry-roasted peanuts**

Lime wedges

1 In a 12-inch skillet heat the oil over medium-high heat. Add mustard seeds and asafetida. Cook and stir for 30 seconds. Add cabbage, carrots, coconut, cilantro, chiles, sugar, and salt. Reduce heat to medium. Cook and stir for 4 to 6 minutes or just until cabbage is cooked. Remove from heat. Stir in lime juice. Transfer to a serving platter. Sprinkle with peanuts. Serve immediately or at room temperature with lime wedges.

*Note: Asafetida is a spice commonly used in Indian cooking. It has a strong odor that fades with cooking and contributes an onionlike flavor.

Nutrition Facts per serving: 290 cal., 20 g total fat (5 g sat. fat), 0 g chol., 621 mg sodium, 24 g carbo., 5 g fiber, 6 g pro.
Daily Values: 179% vit. A, 92% vit. C, 9% calcium, 18% iron

**See note, page 172.

FISH IN MUSTARD SAUCE

Be very careful when adding the mustard-seed mixture to the skillet: You don't want to get burned by the inevitable splatter that occurs when water hits hot oil.

Prep: 15 minutes   **Cook:** 16 minutes   **Makes:** 4 servings

- 1 tablespoon brown mustard seeds, crushed
- 2 cloves garlic, minced
- 1 teaspoon grated fresh ginger
- ½ to 1 small green chile (such as serrano), seeded and finely chopped*
- ½ teaspoon salt
- ½ teaspoon ground turmeric
- ½ teaspoon curry powder
- ½ teaspoon ground fenugreek (optional)
- ½ cup water
- 2 tablespoons cooking oil
- ¼ teaspoon fennel seeds, crushed
- ¼ teaspoon cumin seeds, crushed
- 1 pound cod fillets, cut into 1¼-inch pieces
- 1 recipe Plain Basmati Rice

1 In a small bowl combine mustard seeds, garlic, ginger, chile, salt, turmeric, curry powder, and, if desired, fenugreek. Stir in water; set aside.

2 Heat oil in large nonstick skillet over medium-high heat. Add fennel and cumin seeds. Cook for 10 seconds. Carefully add mustard seed mixture. Bring to boiling; reduce heat. Simmer, uncovered, for 2 minutes. Add fish and return to boiling. Cook and stir for 4 to 6 minutes or until fish flakes easily when tested with a fork. Serve hot with Plain Basmati Rice.

Plain Basmati Rice: Rinse 1 cup uncooked basmati rice as directed on page 179. Drain. In a 2-quart saucepan combine rice and 1¾ cups water. Let stand for 30 minutes. Add 1 tablespoon butter and ½ teaspoon salt. Bring to boiling over medium-high heat; reduce heat. Simmer, covered, for 10 to 15 minutes or until water is absorbed. Fluff rice with fork before serving.

Nutrition Facts per serving: 347 cal., 12 g total fat (3 g sat. fat), 56 mg chol., 678 mg sodium, 34 g carbo., 2 g fiber, 24 g pro. **Daily Values:** 3% vit. A, 4% vit. C, 6% calcium, 18% iron

*See note, page 172.

PEAS AND CARROTS WITH CUMIN

Good friends and good food go together like peas and carrots. Invite a few friends over to take part in an Indian-style feast that includes this colorful vegetable dish.

Start to Finish: 20 minutes   **Makes:** 4 servings

2 **tablespoons cooking oil**	1½ **cups frozen peas**
1 **teaspoon cumin seeds, crushed**	3 **medium carrots, cut into short thin strips**
½ **cup chopped onion**	½ **teaspoon salt**
1 **clove garlic, minced**	**Fresh cilantro leaves**
¼ **teaspoon ground coriander**	
⅛ **to ¼ teaspoon crushed red pepper**	

1 In a large nonstick skillet heat oil over medium heat. Add cumin seeds and cook for 10 seconds. Add onion, garlic, coriander, and crushed red pepper. Cook and stir for 4 to 5 minutes or until onion is tender.

2 Add peas and carrots. Cook and stir for 4 to 6 minutes or until carrots are tender. Stir in salt. Garnish with cilantro.

Nutrition Facts per serving: 131 cal., 7 g total fat (1 g sat. fat), 0 mg chol., 368 mg sodium, 13 g carbo., 4 g fiber, 3 g pro. **Daily Values:** 240% vit. A, 19% vit. C, 3% calcium, 7% iron

KULFI (SAFFRON-PISTACHIO ICE CREAM)

Traditional Indian ice cream, or kulfi, is made with whole milk and a little bit of cream that are both reduced—but you might choose to make the variation, which uses more cream than milk. It's a smooth and cooling treat.

Prep: 5 minutes   **Cook:** 40 minutes   **Chill:** 1 hour   **Freeze:** per manufacturer's directions
Makes: about 3 cups (six ½-cup servings)

4 cups whole milk	1 teaspoon vanilla
⅓ cup sugar	¼ teaspoon ground cardamom
Dash powdered saffron	¼ cup chopped unsalted pistachios
¼ cup whipping cream	

1 In a large saucepan bring milk just to boiling; reduce heat. Simmer, uncovered, for 40 to 45 minutes or until reduced to 1¾ cups, stirring often. (Stir in any film that forms on top.)

2 Stir in sugar; cook and stir for 2 to 3 minutes or until sugar is dissolved. Remove from heat. Stir in saffron. Pour the milk mixture into a bowl. Let cool; cover and chill for 1 hour.

3 Stir in cream, vanilla, and cardamom. Freeze ice cream mixture in a 1-quart ice cream freezer according to manufacturer's instructions. Stir in pistachios. Store in the freezer.

189

Nutrition Facts per serving: 206 cal., 11 g total fat (6 g sat. fat), 36 mg chol., 83 mg sodium, 20 g carbo., 1 g fiber, 6 g pro. **Daily Values:** 8% vit. A, 3% vit. C, 21% calcium, 2% iron

Easy variation: Omit Step 1 and substitute 1¾ cups half-and-half or light cream for the whole milk. Stir together all ingredients except nuts, and freeze as above. Stir in nuts.

Soups and Salads

Callaloo Soup, 197

Mango, Tomato, and Avocado Salad, 203

West Indian Pumpkin Soup, 210

Entrées

Grilled Caribbean Skewers, 213

Island Grilled Tuna and Tropical Fruit, 200

Rum-Glazed Ribs, 204

Caribbean

Side Dishes

Caribbean Rice and Beans, 207

Island Slaw, 206

Skillet Tomatoes and Okra, 212

Tostones with Spicy Mango Mojo, 199

Desserts

Coconut-Orange Tart, 215

Island-Spiced Chocolate Cake, 208

Papayas in Vanilla Syrup, 201

Although immigrants from foreign lands brought many cuisines to the United States, that is not how Caribbean cooking came to this country. Lured by the white sand beaches, cool breezes, and island sunshine, tourists discovered Caribbean cuisine quite by accident, and they couldn't forget the intense seasonings and complex island flavors upon returning home.

Nothing short of exotic, Caribbean cooking reflects a rich history of conquest, slavery, and the occupation of varied cultures. Island Indians, European settlers, African slaves, indentured servants from India and China, and a variety of other island inhabitants added to the cuisine, much the same way cooks add available meat and vegetables to the age-old island dish called pepper pot. While the Arawak and Carib Indians lived off the land and sea, the Europeans (especially the Spanish) imported produce and animals from their homelands to re-create the dishes they loved. Caribbean cooking eventually evolved into a loosely structured fare that lures Americans with its playful spiciness and intriguing blends of ingredients. It would be hard not to love such eclectic, fresh flavors that exude a "no problem" attitude and "every day's a party" energy.

In the '70s, as Bob Marley's famous reggae offered syncopated rhythms over the airwaves and rum cocktails made a splash, more and more Americans made their way to the islands with swimsuits and ready-for-fun attitudes. The tourists actually had to venture off the beaten paths and start dining locally to get the more commercial Caribbean hot spots to stop importing food and start cooking up local fare for travelers. In the last decade or so, island dishes such as jerk chicken and pork, fried plantains, conch chowder, beans and rice, and okra and tomatoes have found their way to America via Caribbean restaurants, cookbooks, and increased imports. Even home cooks are creating jerk chicken for the grill, preparing cooling mango slices, whipping up tropical rum cocktails, and getting into the island spirit at tables in their own kitchens.

papayas

allspice

okra

plantains

mangoes

European explorers from Britain, France, and Spain, African slaves, and traders and settlers from North and South America have left their culinary imprint on the Caribbean region through favored techniques and ingredients both native and imported. Here are some of the favorites.

Allspice is also known as Jamaican pepper and comes from a tree growing only in the New World, most notably the Caribbean, as well as Mexico and Honduras. It acquired the name allspice because its flavor and aroma seem to resemble those of cloves, nutmeg, cinnamon, and black pepper, all together. Moreover, Jamaican jerk seasoning, that popular spice blend from Jamaica, wouldn't be the same without allspice, which, for some, is the signature spice of the blend.

A **plantain** is a quizzical sort of banana that is used as a starchy vegetable. Unlike sweet bananas, plantains are not eaten raw. They become flavorful when cooked, but never sweet like a banana. They are sometimes added to stews, baked, or boiled and are often fried in Spanish-speaking parts of the Caribbean (see Tostones with Spicy Mango Mojo, page 199).

Okra most likely originated in Africa and is thought to have been introduced to the Caribbean—as well as America—by African slaves. Cooks should select smallish okra (approximately 2 to 4 inches long) and those with a bright green color. Larger, older okra can be tough.

Native to eastern Central America, and most likely spreading to the Caribbean by the 16th century, **papaya** is a delicious tropical fruit that is now popular all over the globe. Large, unripe papayas are sometimes cooked as vegetables, but the ripe fruit is juicy and delectable by itself, in salads, and in desserts. Although the black seeds are usually discarded, they are actually edible and sometimes crushed and used as a condiment.

CALLALOO SOUP

Callaloo is the name of the taro root's edible green leaves. A popular green throughout the Caribbean, callaloo is not well-known or widely available in this country. Fresh spinach makes a perfectly acceptable substitute.

Prep: 20 minutes   **Cook:** 25 minutes   **Makes:** 4 servings

- 3 strips thick-sliced bacon, chopped
- ½ cup finely chopped onion
- ¼ cup finely chopped celery
- 1 habañero, Scotch bonnet, or other fresh hot pepper, stemmed, seeded, and minced*
- 1 clove garlic, minced
- 4 14-ounce cans chicken or vegetable broth
- 1 cup sliced fresh or frozen okra
- 12 medium shrimp, peeled and deveined
- 2 cups shredded fresh spinach
  Salt

1 In a large saucepan, cook bacon over medium heat for 5 to 6 minutes or until crisp. Remove bacon from pan with a slotted spoon; set aside. Drain all but 1 tablespoon of the bacon drippings. Add onion, celery, habañero, and garlic to pan. Cook and stir for 4 to 5 minutes or until vegetables are tender.

2 Carefully add broth to pan. Increase heat to medium-high and bring to boiling. Add okra to pan. Reduce heat and simmer, covered, for 10 minutes. Add shrimp and simmer, covered, 5 minutes more or until opaque. Stir in spinach and heat through. Stir in cooked bacon. Season to taste with salt.

Nutrition Facts per serving: 121 cal., 7 g total fat (2 g sat. fat), 40 mg chol., 541 mg sodium, 5 g carbo., 2 g fiber, 9 g pro. **Daily Values:** 21% vit. A, 24% vit. C, 6% calcium, 12% iron

*Note: Because hot peppers, such as habañeros and other chiles, contain volatile oils that can burn your skin and eyes, avoid direct contact with them as much as possible. When working with chile peppers, wear plastic or rubber gloves. If your bare hands do touch the peppers, wash your hands well with soap and water.

TOSTONES WITH SPICY MANGO MOJO

Tostones are fried plantain chips, and "mojo" means "magic" in African slang. Put them together and you have a delicious chip and dip that magically transports you to the islands.

Start to Finish: 45 minutes   **Makes:** 4 servings

¼ **cup finely chopped onion**

1 **tablespoon butter**

1 **medium mango, seeded, peeled, and chopped (1 cup)**

¼ **cup dry white wine**

Several dashes bottled hot pepper sauce

Cooking oil for frying

2 **ripe plantains, peeled* and cut into ½-inch slices**

Salt

1 For sauce, in a small saucepan cook onion in butter over medium heat for 3 to 4 minutes or until tender. Add mango and wine. Bring to boiling; reduce heat. Simmer, uncovered, for 5 minutes. Cool slightly. Place mixture in a food processor bowl or blender container; cover and process or blend until smooth. Add hot pepper sauce to taste. Cool to room temperature.

2 In large saucepan heat 1 inch oil over medium heat to 365°F. (Or use a deep fryer set to 365°F.) Add plantain slices, 4 or 5 at a time, and cook for 2 to 3 minutes until lightly golden, turning them once. Remove plantains with a slotted spoon; drain on paper towels.

3 Transfer plantains to a cutting board. Flatten slices with the bottom of a heavy saucepan to ⅛-inch thickness. (If slices stick to the saucepan, use a wide metal spatula to remove.) Reheat oil, if necessary. Return flattened slices, 4 or 5 at a time, to hot oil and fry for 3 to 4 minutes more or until crisp and deeply golden. Drain on paper towels and sprinkle with salt. Serve tostones warm with dipping sauce.

*Note: Trim off ends and cut a few slits in skin from end to end. Push thumb under skin and peel off in sections.

Nutrition Facts per serving: 342 cal., 21 g total fat (4 g sat. fat), 8 mg chol., 327 mg sodium, 38 g carbo., 3 g fiber, 1 g pro. **Daily Values:** 63% vit. A, 52% vit. C, 1% calcium, 4% iron

199

To peel a plantain, first lay it flat on a cutting board and trim off the ends. Then carefully make several lengthwise slits in the skin.

Peel the skin back along the slits, exposing the fruit. A plantain's skin is only a little tougher than that of an ordinary banana.

ISLAND GRILLED TUNA AND TROPICAL FRUIT

Some believe that a firm-textured, meatier fish such as tuna, marlin, or swordfish, cut into thick steaks, grills even better than beef. You'll love it with sweet fruits and a touch of Caribbean heat.

Prep: 20 minutes   **Grill:** 8 minutes   **Makes:** 4 servings

- 4 4- to 6-ounce fresh or frozen tuna, marlin, or swordfish steaks (about 1 inch thick), thawed if frozen
- 4 slices bacon
- 1 recipe Tropical Glaze
- 4 ½-inch slices fresh pineapple or 4 slices canned, drained pineapple
- 1 small papaya (ripe but firm), peeled, seeded, and quartered
   Lime wedges and thin slices of lemon, orange, and grapefruit peel (optional)

1 Rinse fish; pat dry. In a large skillet cook bacon 2 to 3 minutes or until partially cooked but not crisp. Wrap a piece of bacon around outside of each fish steak and secure with a toothpick.

2 Prepare a grill with a cover for indirect grilling: Arrange preheated coals around a drip pan. Or preheat gas grill, then turn one side off and set drip pan over burners on that side. Test grill for medium heat above pan.

3 Place fish on lightly oiled grill rack over drip pan. Brush with some of the Tropical Glaze. Cover grill and cook for 8 to 12 minutes or just until fish flakes easily with a fork, turning and brushing once with additional glaze halfway through grilling time. Place the pineapple and papaya on the grill rack around the fish and directly over the coals during the last 5 minutes of grilling, turning fruit and brushing once with Tropical Glaze.

4 Bring remaining glaze to boiling in a small saucepan. Drizzle glaze over fish and fruit. If desired, garnish with lime wedges and citrus peels.

Tropical Glaze: In a medium saucepan combine 1 cup pineapple juice, ⅓ cup sugar, 4 teaspoons grated fresh ginger, 1 tablespoon finely shredded lemon peel, ⅓ cup lemon juice, 1 tablespoon cornstarch, and 1 to 2 teaspoons habañero chile sauce or other Caribbean-style hot sauce. Cook and stir until thickened and bubbly. Cook and stir 2 minutes more. Remove from heat and stir in 1 teaspoon vanilla. Makes 1½ cups.

Make-ahead tip: Refrigerate glaze, covered, for up to 1 day.

Nutrition Facts per serving: 374 cal., 11 g total fat (3 g sat. fat), 0 g chol., 158 mg sodium, 38 g carbo., 1 g fiber, 31 g pro. **Daily Values:** 81% vit. C, 11% iron

PAPAYAS IN VANILLA SYRUP

Fresh sweet-tart papaya is delicious in this simple citrus- and vanilla-scented dessert. Serve as is or, better yet, over warm grilled pound cake or shortcake.

Prep: 15 minutes   **Chill:** 4 hours   **Makes:** 6 servings

- 1 **cup sugar**
- 1 **cup water**
- 1 **medium lime**

- ½ **of a vanilla bean or 1 teaspoon vanilla**
- 2 **large papayas, peeled, seeded, and cut into chunks (2 pounds)**

1 In a medium saucepan combine sugar and water. Use a vegetable peeler to remove long, thin strips of peel (green part only) from half of the lime. Add lime peel to sugar mixture; reserve lime for another use. Split vanilla bean, if using, in half lengthwise and scrape out seeds with the back of a knife. Add pod and seeds to sugar mixture. Bring to boiling over medium-high heat, stirring until sugar is dissolved. Remove from heat and let syrup stand for 10 minutes. Discard lime peel and vanilla pod. Stir in vanilla, if using. Place papaya in a medium bowl. Pour syrup over papaya. Cover and chill for at least 4 hours or up to 2 days.

Nutrition Facts per serving: 183 cal., 0 g total fat (0 g sat. fat), 0 mg chol., 8 mg sodium, 45 g carbo., 2g fiber, 0 g pro. **Daily Values:** 6% vit. A, 121% vit. C, 3% calcium, 2% iron

MENU

- Mango, Tomato, and Avocado Salad
- Rum-Glazed Ribs
- Island Slaw
- Caribbean Rice and Beans
- Island-Spiced Chocolate Cake

MANGO, TOMATO, AND AVOCADO SALAD

This beautifully hued salad features fresh tomato, avocado, and mango, the "peach of the tropics." Look for fairly large mangoes—which have a higher fruit-to-seed ratio than smaller ones—and buy only those that are yellow with a blush of red.

Prep: 20 minutes   **Makes:** 4 servings

- 1 **medium mango, seeded, peeled, and cut into chunks**
- 1 **medium tomato, cut into chunks**
- ⅓ **cup thinly sliced red onion**
- 2 **tablespoons snipped fresh cilantro**
- 2 **tablespoons olive oil**
- 1 **tablespoon white wine vinegar**

- 1 **tablespoon lemon juice**
- 1 **clove garlic, minced**
- ¼ **teaspoon salt**
- ⅛ **teaspoon freshly ground black pepper**
- 1 **medium avocado, halved, seeded, peeled, and cut into chunks**
- **Lettuce leaves (optional)**

1 In a medium bowl combine mango, tomato, and red onion.

2 For dressing, in a screw-top jar combine cilantro, olive oil, vinegar, lemon juice, garlic, salt, and pepper. Cover and shake well. Pour dressing over fruit mixture. Toss gently to coat. Cover and chill for up to 4 hours. Stir in avocado just before serving. If desired, serve on lettuce leaves.

203

Nutrition Facts per serving: 166 cal., 12 g total fat (2 g sat. fat), 0 mg chol., 154 mg sodium, 14 g carbo., 3 g fiber, 1 g pro. **Daily Values:** 51% vit. A, 47% vit. C, 2% calcium, 4% iron

RUM-GLAZED RIBS

At the end of the Caribbean's rainbow of colorful drinks lies rum, which also flavors the glaze for these meaty pork ribs.

Prep: 20 minutes **Cook:** 45 minutes **Bake:** 15 minutes **Oven:** 350°F **Makes:** 4 servings

3 pounds pork loin back ribs or meaty pork spareribs
¼ cup mango chutney
⅓ cup bottled chili sauce

2 tablespoons dark rum (optional)
1 clove garlic, minced
½ teaspoon dry mustard
¼ teaspoon salt

1 Cut ribs into serving-size pieces. Place ribs in a 4- to 6-quart Dutch oven. Add enough water to cover. Bring to boiling; reduce heat. Simmer, covered, for 45 minutes or until ribs are tender; drain.

2 Meanwhile, for sauce, snip any large pieces of chutney. In a small bowl stir together chili sauce, chutney, rum (if using), garlic, dry mustard, and salt.

3 Brush some of the sauce over meaty side of ribs. Place ribs, bone sides down, in a shallow roasting pan. Bake, uncovered, in a 350° oven for 15 to 20 minutes or until meat is glazed and heated through. Brush with remaining sauce before serving.

Nutrition Facts per serving: 431 cal., 15 g total fat (5 g sat. fat), 101 mg chol., 504 mg sodium, 19 g carbo., 1 g fiber, 47 g pro. **Daily Values:** 17% vit. A, 20% vit. C, 3% calcium, 11% iron

ISLAND SLAW

There are lots of fruit vinaigrettes on the market with nice, fresh flavors. A tangy orange or tangerine vinaigrette will make this slaw sing.

Start to Finish: 20 minutes   **Makes:** 6 to 8 servings

- 1 16-ounce package shredded cabbage with carrot (coleslaw mix)
- 2 medium papayas, peeled, seeded, and cut into 1-inch pieces
- ½ cup coarsely chopped fresh cilantro
- 2 green onions, thinly sliced (¼ cup)

- 1 or 2 fresh jalapeño peppers, seeded and finely chopped*
- ⅓ cup bottled citrus vinaigrette
  Salt (optional)
  Black pepper (optional)
- 1 lemon, cut in wedges

1 Combine shredded cabbage with carrot, chopped papaya, cilantro, green onions, and jalapeño in a very large mixing bowl. Add vinaigrette; toss to coat. If desired, season with salt and black pepper. Serve immediately with a lemon wedge to squeeze over each serving.

Nutrition Facts per serving: 107 cal., 4 g total fat (1 g sat. fat), 0 mg chol., 169 mg sodium, 21 g carbo., 4 g fiber, 2 g pro.
Daily Values: 117% vit. A, 87% vit. C, 5% calcium, 4% iron

*See note, page 197.

CARIBBEAN RICE AND BEANS

The combination of rice and beans is a staple in much of the world, including Mexico, Cajun country, and the Caribbean, where it's flavored with coconut milk and ground allspice and often called "rice and peas."

Start to Finish: 35 minutes   **Makes:** 4 to 5 servings

- ½ **cup finely chopped onion (1 medium)**
- 2 **cloves garlic, minced**
- 1 **tablespoon butter or margarine**
- ¾ **cup uncooked arborio or short grain rice**
- 1 **14-ounce can vegetable broth or chicken broth**
- 1 **cup purchased unsweetened coconut milk**

- 1 **15½-ounce can small red beans or light red kidney beans, rinsed and drained**
- 1 **fresh jalapeño pepper, chopped***
- 1 **tablespoon snipped fresh thyme or 1 teaspoon dried thyme, crushed**
- ¼ **teaspoon salt**
- ¼ **teaspoon ground allspice**
- ¼ **cup thinly sliced green onions (2)**

1 In a medium saucepan cook the onion and garlic in hot butter until the onion is tender. Add the rice; cook and stir constantly over medium heat about 5 minutes or until rice is golden.

2 Add broth; coconut milk; beans; jalapeño pepper; dried thyme, if using; salt; and allspice. Bring to boiling; reduce heat. Cook, covered, over medium heat for 15 to 20 minutes or until rice is tender and mixture is creamy. Stir in fresh thyme, if using. Sprinkle with green onions.

207

Nutrition Facts per serving: 380 cal., 15 g total fat (11 g sat. fat), 8 mg chol., 913 mg sodium, 52 g carbo., 7 g fiber, 10 g pro. **Daily Values:** 5% vit. A, 9% vit. C, 5% calcium, 21% iron

*See note, page 197.

ISLAND-SPICED CHOCOLATE CAKE

In the Caribbean tradition of generous spicing, a rich chocolate cake is made even better with cinnamon and allspice. Serve this island-style dessert with rum ice cream and a pot of full-bodied coffee.

Prep: 20 minutes   **Stand:** 30 minutes   **Bake:** 40 minutes   **Oven:** 350°F   **Cool:** 2 hours 20 minutes
Makes: 12 servings

½ cup butter
1 cup milk
2 eggs
1⅓ cups all-purpose flour
½ cup unsweetened cocoa powder
¾ teaspoon baking soda
½ teaspoon baking powder
½ teaspoon ground cinnamon

½ teaspoon ground allspice
¼ teaspoon salt
1⅓ cups sugar
1½ teaspoons vanilla
½ cup miniature semisweet chocolate pieces
Whipped cream
Ground cinnamon

1 Allow butter, milk, and eggs to stand at room temperature for 30 minutes. Lightly grease and flour the sides and bottom of a 9-inch springform pan; set aside.

2 In a medium bowl stir together flour, cocoa powder, baking soda, baking powder, the ½ teaspoon cinnamon, the allspice, and salt. Set flour mixture aside.

3 In a large mixing bowl beat butter with an electric mixer on medium to high speed for 30 seconds. Gradually add sugar, about 2 tablespoons at a time, beating on medium speed until well combined (3 to 4 minutes). Scrape sides of bowl; continue beating on medium speed for 2 minutes more. Add eggs 1 at a time, beating after each addition (about 1 minute total). Beat in vanilla.

4 Alternately add flour mixture and milk to butter mixture, beating on low speed after each addition just until combined. Fold in chocolate pieces. Spread batter evenly into prepared pan.

5 Bake in a 350° oven for 40 to 45 minutes or until a wooden toothpick inserted near center comes out clean. Cool cake in pan on a wire rack for 20 minutes. Remove sides of pan. Cool cake completely.

6 To serve, using a serrated knife, cut cake into wedges. Top each serving with a spoonful of whipped cream and sprinkle with additional cinnamon.

Nutrition Facts per serving: 321 cal., 17 g total fat (10 g sat. fat), 79 mg chol., 253 mg sodium, 38 g carbo., 1 g fiber, 4 g pro. **Daily Values:** 12% vit. A, 1% vit. C, 9% calcium, 8% iron

WEST INDIAN PUMPKIN SOUP

You can serve this creamy, richly spiced soup cold or hot. Look for pumpkin seeds (also known as pepitas) at Latin American or Mexican markets. If they're not already roasted, toast the raw seeds in a single layer on a baking sheet for 10 minutes in a 350°F oven.

Prep: 1 hour   **Roast:** 1¼ hours   **Cook:** 40 minutes   **Oven:** 350°F   **Stand:** 10 minutes
Makes: 10 cups

210

- 2 pounds butternut squash or cooking pumpkin, peeled and cut into 1-inch pieces
- 1 pound sweet potatoes, peeled and cut into 1-inch pieces
- 2 tablespoons butter, melted
- 1 tablespoon sugar
- 1 teaspoon kosher salt
- 1 teaspoon freshly ground black pepper
- 2 tablespoons olive oil
- 1 large Spanish onion, chopped
- ½ Scotch bonnet chile or 1 jalapeño pepper, seeded and finely chopped*
- 1 tablespoon minced garlic
- 1 tablespoon grated fresh ginger

- 2 tablespoons snipped fresh thyme or 2 teaspoons dried thyme, crushed
- 2 teaspoons finely grated orange peel
- 1 tablespoon curry powder
- ¼ teaspoon ground nutmeg
- 1 cinnamon stick
- 2 small bay leaves
- 6 cups chicken broth
- ¼ cup whipping cream
- ¼ cup unsweetened coconut milk
- ½ cup pumpkin seeds, toasted
- 2 Granny Smith apples, cored and diced (optional)

1 In a large roasting pan toss together the squash, sweet potatoes, butter, sugar, salt, and black pepper. Roast in a 350° oven for 1 hour and 15 minutes, stirring occasionally, until tender. Set aside.

2 Meanwhile, in a large Dutch oven heat the oil over medium heat. Add onion and cook for 5 minutes. Stir in chile, garlic, and ginger; cook 1 minute more. Add thyme, orange peel, curry, nutmeg, cinnamon stick, and bay leaves. Cook for 1 minute, stirring to coat vegetables. (The mixture will resemble a paste and begin to stick to the bottom of the Dutch oven.) Add the roasted vegetables and any pan liquid, stirring until well combined.

3 Pour in broth and bring to boiling; reduce heat. Simmer, covered, 30 minutes or until vegetables are tender, stirring occasionally. Remove from heat; let stand 10 minutes to cool. Discard cinnamon stick and bay leaves. Place a small amount of soup at a time in a blender container; blend or puree until smooth. Return pureed mixture to Dutch oven. Stir in cream and coconut milk. If desired, cover and refrigerate for up to 24 hours. Serve cold or reheat.

4 To serve, ladle soup into shallow bowls. Sprinkle soup with toasted pumpkin seeds and, if desired, diced apples.

Nutrition Facts per 1-cup serving: 330 cal., 17 g total fat (7 g sat. fat), 21 mg chol., 860 mg sodium, 39 g carbo., 4 g fiber, 8 g pro. **Daily Values:** 256% vit. A, 39% vit. C, 7% calcium, 20% iron

*See note, page 197.

SKILLET TOMATOES AND OKRA

Caribbean cooking features an abundance of okra dishes, a result of its African influence. You can use frozen (then thawed) okra for this vegetable side dish, but fresh okra produces a slightly better texture and flavor.

Start to Finish: 30 minutes   **Makes:** 4 side-dish servings

2 slices bacon	½ teaspoon salt
1 tablespoon butter or margarine	¼ teaspoon freshly ground black pepper
1 small onion, cut into thin wedges	4 small tomatoes, cut into thin wedges
2 cloves garlic, minced	2 teaspoons fresh lime juice
8 ounces whole okra, cut into ½-inch pieces (2 cups)	2 tablespoons snipped fresh basil

1 In a large skillet cook bacon until crisp. Drain bacon on paper towel, reserving 1 tablespoon drippings in skillet. Crumble bacon; set aside.

2 Add butter to drippings in skillet. Cook onion and garlic in hot bacon drippings and butter over medium heat until onion is tender.

3 Stir in okra, salt, and pepper. Cook, covered, over low heat for about 15 minutes or until okra is almost tender. Add tomatoes to skillet. Cook and stir about 3 minutes more or until heated through. Drizzle with lime juice and sprinkle with crumbled bacon and basil.

Nutrition Facts per serving: 126 cal., 8 g total fat (3 g sat. fat), 14mg chol., 400 mg sodium, 11 g carbo., 3 g fiber, 3 g pro. **Daily Values:** 24% vit. A, 54% vit. C, 5% calcium, 6% iron

GRILLED CARIBBEAN SKEWERS

Chunks of turkey, beef sirloin, or lamb all soak up the same brandy-ginger citrus marinade, so it's easy to mix and match the meats. Serve the grill with refreshing Pineapple-Mint Salsa.

Prep: 30 minutes   **Marinate:** 3 hours   **Grill:** 12 minutes   **Makes:** 8 servings

½ cup brandy or orange juice

2 tablespoons olive oil

2 tablespoons brown sugar

1 tablespoon fresh lime juice

1 tablespoon chopped fresh mint

1 tablespoon minced garlic

1 teaspoon grated fresh ginger

1 teaspoon salt

½ teaspoon freshly ground black pepper

½ turkey breast, boned, skinned and cut into 1½-inch cubes (3 pounds), or 2 pounds trimmed boneless beef (sirloin, top round, or chuck) or boneless leg of lamb, cut into 1½-inch cubes

Lemon wedges (optional)

Fresh mint sprigs (optional)

1 For the marinade, in a glass measure combine brandy, olive oil, brown sugar, lime juice, mint, garlic, ginger, salt, and pepper. Pour the mixture into a resealable plastic bag set in a bowl. Add the turkey, seal the bag, and turn the bag to coat the meat in the marinade. Marinate in the refrigerator for 3 hours.

2 Heat grill. On 8 skewers, thread 4 to 5 pieces of turkey or meat. Grill kabobs over medium-hot heat,* 12 to 16 minutes for turkey or until cooked through; or 10 to 12 minutes for medium-rare beef or lamb (145°F). If desired, garnish with lemon wedges and mint sprigs.

*Note: To test for medium-hot heat, you should be able to hold your hand over the coals at the height of the food for 3 seconds before you have to pull it away.

Pineapple-Mint Salsa: In a small saucepan heat 1 tablespoon vegetable oil over medium heat. Add 3 tablespoons minced shallots and cook for 1 minute or until softened. Add one 20-ounce can of crushed pineapple (drained), ¼ cup sugar, and ¼ teaspoon salt; bring to boiling. Cook for 2 minutes, stirring occasionally. Add ¼ cup brandy; cook for 30 seconds. Remove from heat; cool completely. Stir 1 tablespoon fresh mint leaves, chopped, into the salsa.

Make-ahead tip: Marinate turkey, beef, or lamb, covered. Refrigerate up to 24 hours.

Nutrition Facts per serving with 1 tablespoon salsa: 195 cal., 3 g total fat (.5 g sat. fat), 83 mg chol., 230 mg sodium, 7 g carbo., 33 g pro. **Daily Values:** 20% calcium

COCONUT-ORANGE TART

The technique is French, and the flavors are pure tropical. Mixing classic cuisine with Creole touches, the food of the French West Indies still differs from that of other Caribbean islands.

Prep: 30 minutes   **Bake:** 35 minutes   **Oven:** 350°F   **Cool:** 2 hours   **Stand:** 30 minutes
Makes: 12 servings

Almond Pastry	3 oranges
3 eggs, beaten	1 cup chopped fresh pineapple
1 cup sugar	1 cup chopped fresh papaya
⅔ cup flaked coconut	1 tablespoon dark rum or
½ cup all-purpose flour	1 teaspoon vanilla
1½ teaspoons finely shredded orange peel	**Whipped cream (optional)**
1 teaspoon vanilla	**Coconut, toasted (optional)**
¾ cup butter, melted	

1 On a lightly floured surface, use your hands to slightly flatten Almond Pastry dough. Roll dough from center to edges to a circle about 12 inches in diameter. To transfer pastry, wrap it around rolling pin. Unroll pastry into an ungreased 10-inch tart pan with a removable bottom. Ease pastry into tart pan without stretching it. Press pastry into fluted sides of tart pan. Trim edge; set aside.

2 In a large bowl combine eggs, sugar, coconut, flour, orange peel, and vanilla. Slowly stir melted butter into egg mixture until mixed. Pour into the pastry-lined tart pan. Bake in a 350° oven about 35 minutes or until top of tart is crisp. Cool 2 hours in pan on a wire rack. Cover and refrigerate.

3 Peel and section oranges over a medium bowl to catch the juices. Add orange sections, pineapple, papaya, and rum to orange juice. Gently toss to mix fruit. Let stand about 30 minutes.

4 To serve, remove pan sides; cut tart into wedges. Using a slotted spoon, top each wedge with fruit. If desired, top with whipped cream and toasted coconut. Store any leftovers in the refrigerator.

Almond Pastry: In a medium bowl stir together 1¼ cups all-purpose flour, ½ cup ground toasted almonds, and ¼ cup sugar. Using a pastry blender, cut in ½ cup cold butter until the pieces are pea-size. In a small bowl stir together 2 beaten egg yolks and 1 tablespoon water. Gradually stir egg yolk mixture into flour mixture. Using your fingers, gently knead the dough just until a ball forms. If necessary, cover with plastic wrap and chill 30 to 60 minutes or until dough is easy to handle.

Nutrition Facts per 1-cup serving: 435 cal., 27 g total fat (15 g sat. fat), 143 mg chol., 245 mg sodium, 41 g carbo., 2 g fiber, 5 g pro. **Daily Values:** 19% vit. A, 30% vit. C, 4% calcium, 8% iron

The Almond Pastry dough is very easy to handle. Start the rolling pin in the center of the dough, working your way to the outside.

Using the rolling pin is actually the best way to move dough to a tart pan. Roll the dough onto the pin; then ease the dough into the pan.

Mediterranean & Middle Eastern

Appetizers and Salads

Entrées

Side Dishes

Desserts

In the mid-1990s, the Mediterranean Diet was touted as the path to well-being. Although they never gave it such a name, those of Mediterranean and Middle Eastern descent had been enjoying this lauded diet since ancient times—and not only because of its health benefits.

One Moroccan proverb sums it up: "The good supper is known by its odor." The food of the Mediterranean and Middle East (including the Arab states, North Africa, Israel, Turkey, and Greece) is deeply fragrant and flavored with garlic and spices, lemons and herbs, the smoke from an open fire and fruity olive oil.

Because East and West converge in this part of the world, the region has been influenced by many cultures, and the cuisines of its different countries are strikingly similar. Common threads include olive oil and yogurt, marinated and spit-roasted meats, grilled fish and seafood, exquisite salads featuring fresh vegetables and grains, and dips of pureed roasted vegetables and legumes.

The elements of the Mediterranean and Middle Eastern diet that have garnered the most interest in this country, however, are what opens the meal and what ends it. *Mezze* is the Arabic word for appetizers. Hot or cold, simple or elaborate, the vast offering of small bites is dizzying. The Arab legacy has also provided incredible desserts, especially pastries and cakes filled with ground nuts and bathed in sugar syrups perfumed with cinnamon, orange water, and honey. Rice puddings and delicious sweets made with dried or preserved fruits also originated in this part of the world.

"He who eats the sweets of life," says a Lebanese proverb, "should be able to bear the bitters of it."

comb honey

fresh and canned garbanzos, or chickpeas

almonds

fresh mint

couscous

The Middle East and Mediterranean region encompasses so many styles of cooking, it is difficult to identify a single group of ingredients as essential to all. Nonetheless, there are several ingredients that are so closely linked to a particular area's cuisine, or that are so extensively used throughout the region, that they have become important for American cooks to know. The following are only a few.

When we consider biblical references to the Promised Land as "the land of milk and honey" and even earlier evidence that the ancients considered **honey** the food of the gods, not to mention the beekeeping practices of ancient Egyptians, it seems clear that the use of honey in the Middle East is not only long-established but culturally significant as well. From a practical standpoint, cooks should note that different types of honey are usually distinguished by the type of nectar the bees were collecting in order to produce it. For instance, there are popular honeys made from clover, alfalfa, orange blossoms, acacia, heather, and lavender, to name a few. As a general rule, darker-colored honeys are more suitable for cooking, while lighter-hued honeys tend to have more delicate flavors, making them better for use at the table. The subtle flavor and aroma of light honeys are often sacrificed when the honey is heated.

Couscous is so tied to North Africa, and now to America and the rest of the world, that it deserves special attention. The French, in particular, became so enamored of couscous that their name for a special vessel used for cooking it, the *couscoussier*, has stuck with cooks all over the globe. With its pebbly appearance, couscous resembles a whole grain itself, but it is actually made from ground grain—usually semolina, a hard wheat flour.

Chickpeas, known as garbanzos in America, originated in the Middle East, probably as early as 4000 B.C. to 3000 B.C. Their use spread to ancient Greece and, much later, to Spain, which made use of them to help sustain Spanish soldiers and adventurers on the Barbary Coast in the 16th century. In India, chickpea flour, or besan, is commonly used. Today, chickpeas are still used in hummus, a signature dish of the Middle East that has become popular in America. Chickpeas are available both dry and canned.

✦ Menu ✦

Tomato & Onion
Salad

Luleh Kebabs

Rice Vermicelli
Pilaf

Fresh Figs
w/ Yogurt & Honey

TOMATO AND ONION SALAD

The easiest way to seed a tomato is to slice it in half horizontally, exposing all the seed pockets. Scoop out the seeds with a small spoon or turn the tomato upside down and gently squeeze out the seeds. (See photo, page 225.)

Prep: 20 minutes   **Chill:** 1 hour   **Stand:** 30 minutes   **Makes:** 4 to 6 servings

- **4 medium tomatoes, seeded and chopped**
- **1 small onion, halved and thinly sliced**
- **¼ cup snipped fresh parsley**
- **2 tablespoons olive oil**
- **2 tablespoons lemon juice**
- **¼ teaspoon salt**
- **⅛ teaspoon ground black pepper**

1 In a serving bowl combine tomatoes, onion, and parsley.

2 In a small bowl whisk together oil, lemon juice, salt, and pepper. Pour over tomato mixture; lightly toss to combine. Season to taste with additional salt and pepper. Cover and chill for 1 to 2 hours. Let stand at room temperature for 30 minutes before serving.

Nutrition Facts per serving: 94 cal., 7 g total fat (1 g sat. fat), 0 mg chol., 159 mg sodium, 7 g carbo., 1 g fiber, 1 g pro.
Daily Values: 19% vit. A, 55% vit. C, 1% calcium, 5% iron

LULEH KABOBS

Not all kabobs are made with chunks of whole lamb or beef. These Middle Eastern specialties are made with minced or ground meat that's flavored with onion, garlic, fresh herbs, and spices.

Prep: 20 minutes   **Grill:** 16 minutes   **Makes:** 8 servings

¼ cup finely chopped onion

¼ cup finely chopped fresh parsley

1 clove garlic, minced

1 teaspoon salt

½ teaspoon ground coriander

½ teaspoon crushed dried mint leaves (optional)

½ teaspoon freshly ground black pepper

¼ teaspoon ground cumin

1 pound lean ground lamb

½ pound lean ground beef

Pita bread halves

Yogurt-Cucumber Sauce

1 In a large bowl combine onion, parsley, garlic, salt, coriander, mint (if using), pepper, and cumin; add lamb and beef. Mix with hands until well combined and smooth. Using wet hands, form mixture into eight 4×1½-inch logs. Thread logs on skewers. (Or form mixture into ¾-inch patties and omit skewers.)

2 Grill kabobs on the rack of an uncovered grill directly over medium coals for 16 to 18 minutes or until an instant-read thermometer registers 160°F, turning occasionally. (Grill patties for 14 to 18 minutes or until an instant-read thermometer registers 160°F.) Or place kabobs or patties on the unheated rack of a broiler pan; broil 4 inches from heat for 10 to 12 minutes or until an instant-read thermometer registers 160°F, turning once. Serve in pita bread halves with Yogurt-Cucumber Sauce.

Yogurt-Cucumber Sauce: In a small bowl stir together ⅓ cup yogurt, ¼ cup finely chopped cucumber, 1 teaspoon snipped fresh mint or dill (or ¼ teaspoon dried mint, crushed, or dried dill), and a dash of pepper. Cover and refrigerate until serving time.

Nutrition Facts per serving: 243 cal., 10 g total fat (4 g sat. fat), 55 mg chol., 494 mg sodium, 17 g carbo., 1 g fiber, 17 g pro. **Daily Values:** 2% vit. A, 5% vit. C, 4% calcium, 12% iron

RICE VERMICELLI PILAF

Serve this simple rice and pasta pilaf with any variety of grilled or roasted meat or poultry. (See photo, page 225.)

Prep: 10 minutes   **Cook:** 19 minutes   **Makes:** 4 servings

1 **cup long grain white rice**	2 **cups chicken or beef broth**
½ **cup finely broken dried angel hair pasta (2 ounces)**	¼ **teaspoon black pepper**
3 **tablespoons butter**	**Finely snipped fresh parsley**
	Salt and black pepper (optional)

1 In a large saucepan cook rice and angel hair pasta in hot butter over medium heat for 4 to 5 minutes or until pasta is lightly browned. Carefully add broth and pepper; bring to boiling. Reduce heat. Simmer, covered, for 15 to 20 minutes or until the rice is tender and broth is absorbed. Fluff rice with a fork and, if desired, season to taste with salt and pepper; sprinkle with parsley before serving.

Nutrition Facts per serving: 322 cal., 10 g total fat (6 g sat. fat), 24 mg chol., 484 mg sodium, 48 g carbo., 1 g fiber, 7 g pro. **Daily Values:** 8% vit. A, 2% vit. C, 2% calcium, 16% iron

FRESH FIGS WITH YOGURT AND HONEY

Although people of Arab descent are known for their fondness for intensely sweet desserts, for many Mediterraneans, dessert is often made up of the healthier sweets: fresh fruit, nuts, and soft cheese.

Prep: 15 minutes   **Chill:** 8 hours   **Makes:** 4 servings

- 16 ounces plain yogurt
- 12 fresh figs, halved lengthwise (quarter large figs)
- ¼ cup coarsely chopped walnuts, lightly toasted
- ¼ cup honey
- Finely shredded lemon peel (optional)

1 Place yogurt in a mesh or paper coffee filter or a cheesecloth-lined strainer over a glass measure. Cover and refrigerate overnight or up to 24 hours. Yogurt will thicken and form a soft cheese.

2 In a small bowl gently stir together the yogurt cheese, figs, and nuts. Spoon the mixture into two bowls. Drizzle each serving with honey and, if desired, sprinkle with lemon peel.

Nutrition Facts per serving: 300 cal., 7 g total fat (1 g sat. fat), 6 mg chol., 75 mg sodium, 56 g carbo., 5 g fiber, 7 g pro. **Daily Values:** 6% vit. A, 7% vit. C, 25% calcium, 5% iron

Menu

Baba Ghanoush

North African
LAMB Stew

Heavenly Couscous

Honey Pistachio
Tart

BABA GHANOUSH

This eggplant and tahini dip, infused with lemon and garlic, satisfies taste buds across the Middle East. It's just one of the many "little dishes" that make up the mezze, or appetizer table, of the Arab world.

Prep: 15 minutes   **Bake:** 25 minutes   **Oven:** 400°F   **Makes:** 2 cups (32 1-tablespoon servings)

1 **large eggplant (about 1½ pounds)**	1 **teaspoon minced garlic**
2 **tablespoons fresh lemon juice**	1 **teaspoon salt**
2 **tablespoons tahini (sesame paste)**	2 **tablespoons chopped fresh parsley**
1 **tablespoon olive oil**	**Toasted pitas**

1 Halve the eggplant lengthwise and place, cut sides down, on a baking sheet lined with foil. Prick skin all over with a fork. Bake in a 400° oven for 25 minutes or until tender when pierced with a fork.

2 Use a small knife to remove eggplant skin. Transfer pulp to a food processor or blender; add the lemon juice, tahini, olive oil, garlic, and salt. Process or blend until smooth.

3 Transfer dip to a bowl and stir in the parsley. Serve with toasted pitas.

Nutrition Facts per tablespoon dip plus ⅛-section of pita: 35 cal., 1 g total fat (0 g sat. fat), 0 mg chol., 113 mg sodium, 5 g carbo., 1 g pro. **Daily Values:** 1% vit. A, 2% vit. C, 1% calcium, 2% iron

NORTH AFRICAN LAMB STEW

Native Moroccans call this dish *tagine.* That's their term for any stew that's slowly simmered with vegetables and lots of spices and served over couscous.

Prep: 40 minutes   **Cook:** 1 hour 20 minutes   **Makes:** 4 servings

1 pound boneless lamb shoulder or leg, cut into 1½-inch cubes
½ teaspoon salt
2 tablespoons cooking oil
1 large onion, sliced
2 teaspoons grated fresh ginger
½ teaspoon ground cumin
¼ teaspoon ground cinnamon
¼ teaspoon crushed red pepper

1½ cups Lamb Stock or beef broth or water
1 medium sweet potato, peeled and cut into 1-inch cubes (8 ounces)
1 cup canned garbanzo beans, rinsed and drained
1 cup canned fava beans, rinsed and drained
2 cups hot cooked couscous

1 Sprinkle the meat with salt; toss to coat. In a large saucepan or Dutch oven brown meat, half at a time, in 1 tablespoon of the hot oil; remove from pan.

2 Add onion and the remaining 1 tablespoon of oil to the pan. Cook and stir until onion is golden brown. Stir in ginger, cumin, cinnamon, and red pepper. Return meat to the pan; add the Lamb Stock. Bring to boiling; reduce heat. Simmer, covered, for 1 hour, stirring occasionally.

3 Stir in sweet potato. Return to boiling; reduce heat. Simmer, covered, 20 minutes or until meat and sweet potato are tender. Stir in beans; heat through. Serve with couscous.

Lamb Stock: To make lamb stock, which is better than beef stock for this recipe, use your favorite beef stock or broth recipe and substitute lamb bones for the beef bones.

Nutrition Facts per serving: 504 cal., 15 g total fat (3 g sat. fat), 74 mg chol., 1,079 mg sodium, 57 g carbo., 12 g fiber, 33 g pro. **Daily Values:** 205% vit. A, 26% vit. C, 9% calcium, 20% iron

HEAVENLY COUSCOUS

The term couscous refers to both the grain—a type of tiny pasta—and the finished dish. Couscous derives from the French pronunciation of the North African word *suksoo*, which in theory describes the sound steam makes as it passes through the cooking grains. Top with meat or chicken, or mix with dried fruits and nuts and serve as an accompaniment to stew.

Start to Finish: 15 minutes   **Makes:** 4 servings

1 cup dried couscous
¼ teaspoon salt
1 cup boiling water
1 teaspoon butter

¼ cup slivered almonds
¼ cup snipped dried apricots
½ teaspoon finely shredded orange peel

1 In a medium bowl mix couscous and salt. Gradually add boiling water. Let stand until liquid is absorbed, about 5 minutes.

2 Meanwhile, in a small skillet over medium heat melt butter. Add almonds; stir until almonds are light golden brown. Remove almonds from skillet to cool. Fluff couscous with a fork. Add apricots, orange peel, and toasted almonds. Fluff again. Serve immediately.

Nutrition Facts per serving: 250 cal., 5 g total fat (1 g sat. fat), 2 mg chol., 163 mg sodium, 42 g carbo., 4 g fiber, 8 g pro.
Daily Values: 13% vit. A, 1% vit. C, 4% calcium, 7% iron

HONEY-PISTACHIO TART

The flavor of this dried fruit and nut tart varies, depending on the type of honey you use to make it. A delicate floral honey, such as one made from orange blossoms, works well here.

Prep: 25 minutes   **Bake:** 35 minutes   **Oven:** 375°F   **Makes:** 8 to 12 servings

½ **cup sugar**	¼ **teaspoon salt**
¼ **cup honey**	⅔ **cup vegetable shortening**
¼ **cup water**	1 **egg**
1½ **cups chopped pistachio nuts, toasted**	¼ **cup cold water**
½ **cup mixed dried fruit bits**	1 **beaten egg yolk**
¼ **cup orange juice**	**Coarse sugar**
2 **cups all-purpose flour**	

1 For filling, in a medium saucepan stir together sugar, honey, and the ¼ cup water. Bring to boiling, stirring until sugar is dissolved. Reduce heat to medium low. Gently simmer, uncovered, for 15 minutes or until liquid is a light caramel color, stirring occasionally. Stir in pistachios, fruit, and orange juice. Return to boiling; reduce heat. Simmer, uncovered, for 5 minutes or until mixture is slightly thickened, stirring occasionally. Set aside.

2 For egg pastry, in a large bowl combine flour and salt. Using a pastry blender, cut in shortening until pieces are pea-size. In a small bowl beat together egg and the ¼ cup cold water. Add egg mixture to flour mixture. Using a fork, toss until dry ingredients are moistened. Divide dough in half. Form each half into a ball.

3 Slightly flatten one ball of egg pastry into a rectangle. On a lightly floured surface roll dough into a 16×6-inch rectangle. Wrap pastry around a rolling pin. Unroll onto a 13½×4-inch rectangular tart pan with a removable bottom. Ease pastry into pan, pressing it up the fluted sides. Trim pastry even with top edge of pan. Spoon filling evenly into crust.

4 For top pastry, roll out remaining pastry ball into a 10-inch square. Using a fluted pastry wheel, cut strips ½ inch wide. Diagonally weave strips across top of filling for a lattice; press ends into rim of pan. Brush egg yolk over lattice and sprinkle with sugar.

5 Bake at 375° for about 35 minutes or until top is golden. (If crust begins to brown quickly, cover with foil.) Cool in pan on a wire rack. Remove sides from pan.

Nutrition Facts per serving: 523 cal., 30 g total fat (6 g sat. fat), 53 mg chol., 84 mg sodium, 57 g carbo., 3 g fiber, 9 g pro. **Daily Values:** 9% vit. C, 3% calcium, 21% iron

233

Menu

Lemony Herbed Olives

Blood Orange & Walnut Salad

Classic Potato Latkes

Stuffed Beef Brisket

Sweet Apple Noodle Kugel

LEMONY HERBED OLIVES

Never underestimate the importance of these small oily fruits to Mediterranean and Middle Eastern cultures. Moroccans savor them with chicken and preserved lemons, Provençals pound them into a delectable paste called tapenade, and Greeks eat them with just about everything.

Prep: 15 minutes   **Marinate:** 4 hours   **Stand:** 30 minutes   **Makes:** 56 appetizer servings

1 **pound pitted kalamata olives and/or green olives (3½ cups)**	2 **teaspoons snipped fresh oregano or ½ teaspoon dried oregano, crushed**
1 **tablespoon olive oil**	½ **to 1 teaspoon crushed red pepper**
½ **teaspoon finely shredded lemon peel**	**Lemon peel curls (optional)**
1 **tablespoon lemon juice**	

1 Place olives in a plastic bag set in a shallow bowl. For marinade, combine olive oil, lemon peel, lemon juice, oregano, and crushed red pepper. Pour over olives; close bag. Marinate in the refrigerator for 4 to 24 hours, turning bag occasionally.

2 To serve, let olives stand at room temperature for 30 minutes. Drain and serve. If desired, garnish olives with curled strips of lemon peel.

235

Nutrition Facts per appetizer serving: 21 cal., 1 g total fat (0 g sat. fat), 0 mg chol., 135 mg sodium, 1 g carbo., 0 g fiber, 0 g pro.

BLOOD ORANGE AND WALNUT SALAD

Here's fruit salad the Moroccan way. North Africans often serve salads that feature oranges (and sometimes dates) as a refreshing and cooling counterpoint to heavily spiced foods.

Start to Finish: 15 minutes   **Makes:** 4 servings

¼ **cup olive oil**

2 **tablespoons frozen orange juice concentrate, thawed**

1 **tablespoon white wine vinegar**

2 **teaspoons snipped fresh mint**

1 **teaspoon honey**

Dash salt

4 **cups purchased torn mixed spring salad greens**

2 **medium blood or navel oranges, peeled and sectioned**

¼ **cup chopped walnuts, toasted***

Fresh mint leaves for garnish (optional)

1 In a screw-top jar combine oil, orange juice concentrate, white wine vinegar, snipped mint, honey, and salt. Cover and shake well; set aside.

2 Place greens on salad plates. Drizzle half of the dressing over the greens. Toss to combine. Top with orange sections and walnuts. If desired, garnish with fresh mint leaves. Pass remaining dressing.

***Note:** To toast nuts, spread nuts in a shallow baking pan. Bake in a 350°F oven for 5 to 10 minutes or until light golden brown, watching carefully and stirring once or twice to prevent the nuts from burning.

Nutrition Facts per serving: 210 cal., 18 g total fat (2 g sat. fat), 0 mg chol., 40 mg sodium, 10 g carbo., 2 g fiber, 2 g pro. **Daily Values:** 5% vit. A, 54% vit. C, 3% calcium, 4% iron

237

CLASSIC POTATO LATKES

To render the chicken fat, or schmaltz, that makes these potato cakes so flavorful, remove the fat and skin from a whole chicken. Wash it, dry it, and cut it into pieces to measure 1 cup. Cook it in a heavy skillet, uncovered, with ¼ cup sliced onion and ¼ cup salted water for about 30 minutes or until fat is completely melted. Strain the melted fat through cheesecloth into a container. You can refrigerate or freeze the schmaltz for future use.

Prep: 30 minutes   **Cook:** 6 minutes per batch   **Makes:** about 10 latkes

- 4 medium potatoes (about 1½ pounds)
- 3 tablespoons rendered chicken fat (schmaltz)
- 2 slightly beaten eggs
- 2 cloves garlic, finely minced
- ½ teaspoon salt
- 2 tablespoons cooking oil
- Sour cream (optional)

1 Peel and finely shred potatoes. In a large bowl combine potatoes, chicken fat, eggs, garlic, and salt. Using ⅓ cup mixture for each latke, press mixture into patties about the size of the palm of your hand (about 2½ inches in diameter), squeezing out excess liquid.

2 In a large skillet heat oil over medium-high heat. Carefully slide patties into hot oil. Cook over medium-high heat about 2 minutes or until latkes are golden brown, turning once. Repeat with remaining patties, adding more oil during cooking as needed. If necessary, reduce heat to medium to prevent overbrowning. Drain on paper towels; keep warm. If desired, serve with sour cream.

Nutrition Facts per latke: 131 cal., 8 g total fat (2 g sat. fat), 46 mg chol., 167 mg sodium, 12 g carbo., 1 g fiber, 3 g pro.
Daily Values: 88% vit. C, 2% iron

238

STUFFED BEEF BRISKET

Sliced spirals of this roasted brisket show off an exotic stuffing of brandy-soaked dried figs, leeks, fresh pear, and toasted pecans.

Prep: 50 minutes   **Stand:** 15 minutes   **Bake:** 40 minutes   **Oven:** 375°F   **Makes:** 8 servings

½ cup chopped dried figs or prunes (3 ounces)

¼ cup brandy or water

1 large leek, white and pale green part only, or 1 medium onion, chopped (½ cup)

2 teaspoons olive oil

1 small pear, cored and finely chopped

2 cloves garlic, minced

¼ cup chopped pecans, toasted

2 tablespoons fine matzo crumbs

1 teaspoon finely shredded lemon peel

½ teaspoon dried thyme, crushed

¼ to ½ teaspoon coarsely ground black pepper

1 2- to 2¼-pound beef brisket

Salt

Ground black pepper

2 tablespoons olive oil

1 In a small saucepan place dried fruit and brandy. Heat over low heat just until hot (do not boil). Remove from heat, cover, and let stand for 15 to 20 minutes or until fruit is plumped and most of the liquid is absorbed. Drain fruit, reserving liquid.

2 Meanwhile, in a medium skillet cook leek in the 2 teaspoons oil until tender. Add reserved brandy liquid, the pear, and garlic; cook and stir until tender. Add softened fruit, pecans, matzo crumbs, lemon peel, thyme, and ¼ to ½ teaspoon black pepper; stir to combine.

3 Make a horizontal cut through the beef brisket, splitting it almost in half but leaving meat intact on one side; spread brisket open. Using the flat side of a meat mallet, lightly pound the entire surface to about ½-inch thickness. Season lightly with salt and additional pepper. Spread fruit mixture over meat to within ½ inch of edges. Starting from a long edge, roll up meat and fruit mixture; tie with kitchen string at 1-inch intervals.

4 In a large skillet or Dutch oven brown meat in the 2 tablespoons oil. Place brisket in a roasting pan on an oven rack. Bake in a 375° oven about 40 minutes or until a meat thermometer inserted near center of meat registers 140°. Transfer to a platter; cover with foil. Let stand for 10 minutes before slicing and serving (temperature will rise 5° during standing).

Nutrition Facts per serving: 465 cal., 35 g total fat (12 g sat. fat), 65 mg chol., 65 mg sodium, 14 g carbo., 2 g fiber, 20 g pro. **Daily Values:** 3% vit. C, 3% calcium, 13% iron

239

SWEET APPLE NOODLE KUGEL

Two versions of the hearty noodle pudding known as kugel exist: one sweet, one savory. Both fit into a traditional Jewish Sabbath meal.

Prep: 30 minutes   **Bake:** 55 minutes   **Oven:** 350°F   **Cool:** 30 minutes   **Makes:** 12 servings

12 ounces dried wide noodles	¾ cup sugar
4 medium cooking apples, such as Jonathan, Braeburn, or Granny Smith, peeled, cored, and thinly sliced (4 cups)	2 tablespoons honey
	2 teaspoons ground cinnamon
	1 teaspoon vanilla
2 tablespoons margarine or cooking oil	½ cup dried tart cherries or raisins
2 cups apple juice	½ cup chopped pecans
4 beaten eggs	

1 In a large saucepan or Dutch oven cook noodles according to package directions. Drain, rinse, and drain again; set aside.

2 In a large skillet cook apples in hot margarine over medium heat for 3 minutes; set aside. In a large bowl whisk together the apple juice, eggs, sugar, honey, cinnamon, and vanilla. Layer half of the noodles in a lightly greased 3-quart rectangular baking dish. Top with the apples and cherries. Cover with remaining noodles. Sprinkle pecans on the noodles. Pour apple juice mixture over all. Cover dish with foil.

3 Bake at 350° for 40 minutes. Uncover and bake 15 minutes more. Cool on a wire rack about 30 minutes. Serve warm.

Nutrition Facts per serving: 305 cal., 8 g total fat (1 g sat. fat), 98 mg chol., 48 mg sodium, 52 g carbo., 3 g fiber, 7 g pro.
Daily Values: 5% vit. C, 3% calcium, 10% iron

~Menu~

Spanakopita

chicken Souvlaki

Tossed Green Salad*

Baklava

*Supplement this Greek-inspired meal with a simple green
salad of lettuce, tomato, kalamata olives, and feta cheese.
Toss with a favorite oil-and-vinegar dressing.

SPANAKOPITA

During the required 30-minute "chill," you can clean up the kitchen and chill out with your favorite beverage. Afterward, this classic Greek spinach-and-cheese main-dish pastry bakes to crisp perfection.

Prep: 30 minutes   **Chill:** 30 minutes   **Bake:** 45 minutes   **Oven:** 375°F   **Stand:** 15 minutes
Makes: 8 to 10 servings

2 tablespoons extra-virgin olive oil	1 large egg, beaten
2 large onions, finely chopped	2 tablespoons chopped fresh dill
Water	2 tablespoons fresh lemon juice
1½ teaspoons salt	Freshly ground black pepper
3 10-ounce boxes frozen chopped spinach	16 sheets phyllo dough (12×17 inches each)
3 cups large-curd cottage cheese	½ cup unsalted butter, melted
8 ounces feta cheese	

1 Heat oil in a large nonstick skillet over medium heat. Add onions and cook for 5 minutes or until translucent. In a large saucepan with 1 inch of water and ½ teaspoon of the salt place the spinach. Cook, covered, about 10 minutes or until wilted and hot. Drain spinach in a colander and press out as much water as possible.

2 In a large bowl combine the onions, spinach, cottage cheese, feta cheese, egg, dill, lemon juice, the remaining 1 teaspoon salt, and pepper to taste.

3 In a greased 9×13-inch baking dish place 1 phyllo sheet. (Cover remaining phyllo with plastic wrap and a clean kitchen towel.) Lightly brush phyllo sheet in baking dish with melted butter. Layer and spread melted butter on 7 more phyllo sheets. Spread the spinach mixture on the phyllo. Place 1 phyllo sheet over top and brush with butter. Repeat with remaining phyllo sheets. Roll up overhanging phyllo on the sides to form a crust. With a sharp knife, cut the pie into squares or diamonds without cutting through the bottom. Refrigerate for 30 minutes.

4 Bake at 375° for 45 minutes or until crisp and golden brown. Let stand for 15 minutes. To serve, cut through the bottom layer.

Nutrition Facts per serving: 457 cal., 28 g total fat (15 g sat. fat), 96 mg chol., 1,263 mg sodium, 31 g carbo., 4 g fiber, 21 g pro. **Daily Values:** 172% vit. A, 30% vit. C, 32% calcium, 21% iron

CHICKEN SOUVLAKI

Skewered souvlaki is to Greece what the kabob is to the rest of the Middle East: chunks of marinated meat or poultry threaded on a stick and cooked over a smoky fire.

Prep: 25 minutes   **Marinate:** 3 hours   **Broil:** 10 minutes   **Makes:** 4 servings

- 1 pound skinless, boneless chicken thighs or breasts
- 1/3 cup oil-and-vinegar salad dressing
- 1 teaspoon finely shredded lemon peel
- 1 tablespoon lemon juice
- 1 teaspoon snipped fresh rosemary or 1/4 teaspoon dried rosemary, crushed
- 1 teaspoon snipped fresh thyme or 1/4 teaspoon dried thyme, crushed
- 2 small green sweet peppers, cut into 1-inch pieces
- 1 medium onion, cut into 8 wedges
- 3 cups hot cooked rice

1 Cut chicken into 1-inch pieces. Place chicken in a plastic bag set in a shallow bowl.

2 For marinade, combine salad dressing, lemon peel, lemon juice, rosemary, and thyme. Pour over chicken; close bag. Marinate in the refrigerator for 3 to 24 hours, turning bag occasionally.

3 Drain chicken, reserving marinade. On eight 8-inch skewers* alternately thread chicken, green peppers, and onion. Brush peppers and onion with reserved marinade. Place kabobs on the unheated rack of a broiler pan. Broil 3 to 4 inches from heat for 10 to 12 minutes or until chicken is tender and no longer pink, turning once. (Or grill on the rack of an uncovered grill directly over medium heat for 10 to 12 minutes, turning once.) Serve with rice.

*Note: If desired, use rosemary sticks for skewers. Be sure to soak the sticks in water for 1 hour before making the kabobs.

Nutrition Facts per serving: 392 cal., 17 g total fat (3 g sat. fat), 54 mg chol., 337 mg sodium, 41 g carbo., 1 g fiber, 20 g pro. **Daily Values:** 90% vit. C, 2% calcium, 17% iron

BAKLAVA

Though baklava is attributed to the Greeks, some form of this syrup-soaked, nutty pastry is eaten with great enthusiasm throughout the eastern Mediterranean.

Prep: 50 minutes   **Cook:** 30 minutes   **Bake:** 40 minutes   **Oven:** 325°F   **Makes:** 35 servings

1¼ cups sugar
1 cup water
2 to 3 inches stick cinnamon
½ teaspoon finely shredded lemon peel
½ cup honey
2 tablespoons brandy (or 1 tablespoon brandy and 1 tablespoon rum) (optional)
1 tablespoon fresh lemon juice

16 ounces walnuts, very finely ground (3 cups)
½ cup sugar
2 tablespoons ground cinnamon
½ teaspoon ground nutmeg
1½ cups unsalted butter, melted
1 16-ounce package phyllo dough (9×14-inch sheets), thawed

1 For syrup, in a medium saucepan stir together the 1¼ cups sugar, water, cinnamon stick, and lemon peel. Bring to boiling; reduce heat. Simmer, uncovered, over medium heat for 30 minutes, stirring occasionally. Remove from heat. Stir in honey, brandy, and lemon juice. Strain syrup to remove lemon peel and cinnamon. Let syrup cool to room temperature (do not refrigerate).

2 For filling, in a large bowl stir together walnuts, the ½ cup sugar, ground cinnamon, and nutmeg. Set aside.

3 Brush the bottom of a 3-quart baking dish with some of the melted butter. Unfold phyllo dough. With kitchen shears or a knife cut through the whole stack of phyllo dough sheets at one time to make a 13×9-inch rectangle. Discard extra pieces. Keep phyllo covered with plastic wrap, removing sheets as you need them. One layer at a time, layer 10 phyllo sheets in the dish, generously brushing each sheet with melted butter. Sprinkle one-third (about 1⅓ cups) of the filling on the phyllo layers. Repeat layering the phyllo sheets and filling twice. Layer remaining phyllo sheets on the third layer of filling, brushing each sheet with butter before layering the next sheet. Drizzle any remaining butter on the top layer.

4 With a sharp knife, make 4 cuts through all layers the length of the dish to make 5 rows. Then make 8 diagonal cuts through all layers, making diamonds. (Do not remove from dish.) Bake in a 325° oven for 40 to 50 minutes or until golden. Slightly cool in baking dish on a wire rack. Spoon syrup over hot baklava. Cool completely or let stand overnight at room temperature before serving.

Nutrition Facts per serving: 294 cal., 20 g total fat (7 g sat. fat), 26 mg chol., 75 mg sodium, 26 g carbo., 1 g fiber, 3 g pro.
Daily Values: 7% vit. A, 1% vit. C, 3% calcium, 6% iron

Gently layer the phyllo to avoid tearing. Keep remaining phyllo covered until needed.

Each layer of phyllo must be brushed with melted butter to make the flakiest, tastiest baklava.

Cajun & Creole

247

If you have an *envie*—a yearning—for good eating, look for the nearest roux pot, the Cajuns would say. If you think there's a place in America that is more about eating well and enjoying life than southern Louisiana is, you'll be in for a lively argument to assert so. This is the land of crawfish feasts and dances that start in the morning and last deep into the night.

New Orleans was established as a French town in the late 17th century. In the mid-18th century the French turned the territory over to the Spanish, who imported 1,600 Acadians from France. Originally citizens of French Nova Scotia, the Acadians had been driven from their homeland by the conquering British. The Native Americans of the territory mispronounced Acadian as Cajun, and the name stuck.

New Orleans and its surrounding area are known for two types of cooking: Cajun and Creole. Cajun cooking originated in the bayou country west and south of the Crescent City. It is country food that utilizes fiery flavors and an abundance of animal fat. Creole cooking is more refined, "city" food that emphasizes the use of cream and butter as well as lots of tomatoes, green peppers, onions, and garlic.

Cajun and Creole cooking are more similar than different, though, thanks to the influence of the immigrant groups who followed the French and the Spanish, and to that of African-American plantation cooks. Both cuisines were built on a French foundation, enlivened with Spanish spices, freshened with African vegetables, made rich with German pork fat, made fiery with West Indian peppers, and infused with Italian garlic and tomatoes.

Both types of cooking may be rich, but eat them the traditional way, with a zydeco band playing nearby, and you are sure to dance it off.

dry black-eyed peas

pecans

black, white, and cayenne pepper

andouille sausage

From hearty meats to subtle seafood, from exotic seasonings to down-home beans and vegetables, Cajun and Creole ingredients reflect the spicy, soulful character of life in a unique American region.

In addition to the traditional green sweet peppers, onions, and celery that are included in many dishes, a trio of spices—**white, black, and red (cayenne) pepper**—is also a key to these regional cuisines. White and black pepper are the cracked or crushed peppercorns from the same plant, with black pepper having a slightly stronger bite and flavor. The white form is given a longer ripening time, which mellows its flavor. Red pepper, or cayenne, on the other hand, is ground from dried hot, red chile peppers.

Crawfish (or crayfish) are of huge symbolic and culinary value to Louisiana as a whole. The eating of this freshwater relative of the lobster dates back to medieval France, in which country they are still popular today. Most crawfish are fairly small—no more than 6 to 8 inches long—although the Tasmanian crayfish has been known to attain a weight of almost 10 pounds! Crawfish are most often boiled or stewed.

Another symbol of the region is **Tabasco sauce**. Tabasco is actually a trade name for a hot chile pepper sauce that has been made on Avery Island in Louisiana since at least the 1870s. Its distinctive flavor is often attributed to a fermentation process the peppers go through as they spend years curing in barrels before being processed into sauce.

Andouille is a very smoky, very spicy pork sausage that adds flavor and richness to many gumbo and jambalaya recipes. Like quite a few Cajun and Creole techniques and ingredients, this one too comes from France. Authentic French andouille is a similarly highly smoky sausage, spending 2 months over beech wood smoke.

A key thickening and flavoring ingredient, **filé powder** (also known as gumbo filé) is made from leaves of the sassafras tree, dried and ground to a powder.

MENU

PECAN-CRUSTED CATFISH

RICE
w/ ANDOUILLE SAUSAGE
AND PEPPERS

HUSH PUPPIES

NUTMEG BEIGNETS
OR SOUTHERN PECAN PIE

PECAN-CRUSTED CATFISH

Up the ante at a Friday night fish fry: Serve this crunchy catfish with cold beverages and hot Cajun music.

Prep: 20 minutes   **Cook:** 3 minutes   **Makes:** 4 servings

Cooking oil for deep-fat frying
½ cup buttermilk
¼ cup finely chopped fresh chives
1 tablespoon dry mustard
1 cup ground pecans

1 cup fine dry bread crumbs
1 teaspoon salt
1 pound catfish chunks or nuggets or fillets cut into 2-inch pieces
Lemon wedges

1 In a large saucepan or deep fryer heat 3 to 4 inches of oil to 365°F.

2 In a shallow bowl combine the buttermilk, chives, and mustard. In another shallow dish combine pecans, bread crumbs, and salt. Dip the catfish in the buttermilk mixture, then coat it with the pecan mixture.

3 Fry fish pieces, 3 at a time, about 3 minutes or until fish flakes easily when tested with a fork, turning once. Drain on paper towels. Serve with lemon wedges.

Nutrition Facts per 1-cup serving: 554 cal., 43 g total fat (6 g sat. fat), 54 mg chol., 1,205 mg sodium, 20 g carbo., 3 g fiber, 23 g pro. **Daily Values:** 4% vit. A, 5% vit. C, 12% calcium, 14% iron

RICE WITH ANDOUILLE SAUSAGE AND PEPPERS

Andouille sausage is one part European, one part southern Louisiana. Although its name is French, its spicy flavor comes from the hot peppers that flourish in the Louisiana heat.

Prep: 20 minutes   **Bake:** 50 minutes   **Oven:** 350°F   **Makes:** 4 servings

¼ cup chopped onion

1 tablespoon cooking oil

¾ cup uncooked long grain rice

1½ cups chicken broth

1 tablespoon snipped fresh celery leaves

1 teaspoon paprika

¼ teaspoon salt

¼ teaspoon dried thyme, crushed

6 ounces andouille sausage, halved lengthwise and cut into ½-inch slices (about 1 cup)

½ cup chopped red and/or green sweet peppers

¼ cup chopped green onion

1 In a large skillet cook onion in hot oil over medium heat until tender. Add rice; cook and stir until rice is golden.

2 Meanwhile, in a small saucepan combine broth, celery leaves, paprika, salt, and thyme. Bring to boiling; remove from heat.

3 In a greased 1-quart casserole combine the rice mixture and chicken broth mixture. Stir in sausage and sweet peppers. Cover and bake in a 350° oven for 50 to 60 minutes or until rice is tender. Sprinkle with green onion.

Nutrition Facts per serving: 350 cal., 17 g total fat (5 g sat. fat), 29 mg chol., 1,078 mg sodium, 32 g carbo., 1 g fiber, 14 g pro. **Daily Values:** 30% vit. A, 66% vit. C, 4% calcium, 15% iron

HUSH PUPPIES

For the crispest, lightest results, fry only five or six hush puppies at a time so the oil temperature doesn't drop too low. Heat the oil back to 375°F before adding more hush puppies.

Prep: 10 minutes   **Fry:** 3 minutes per batch   **Makes:** 14 to 18 hush puppies

1 **cup cornmeal**	1 **beaten egg**
¼ **cup all-purpose flour**	½ **cup buttermilk or sour milk***
2 **teaspoons sugar**	¼ **cup sliced green onions (2)**
¾ **teaspoon baking powder**	**Shortening or cooking oil for deep-fat frying**
¼ **teaspoon baking soda**	
¼ **teaspoon salt**	

1 In a medium bowl stir together the cornmeal, flour, sugar, baking powder, baking soda, and salt. Make a well in the center of the flour mixture; set aside.

2 In another bowl combine the egg, buttermilk, and green onions. Add the egg mixture all at once to the flour mixture. Stir just until moistened (batter should be lumpy).

3 Drop batter by tablespoons into deep, hot shortening (375°F). Fry about 3 minutes or until golden, turning once. Drain on paper towels. Serve warm.

*Note: To make sour milk, for each cup of sour milk needed, place 1 tablespoon lemon juice or vinegar in a glass measure. Add enough milk to make 1 cup total liquid; stir. Let the mixture stand for 5 minutes before using.

Nutrition Facts per hush puppy: 95 cal., 5 g total fat (1 g sat. fat), 15 mg chol., 100 mg sodium, 11 g carbo., 1 g fiber, 2 g pro. **Daily Values:** 1% vit. A, 1% vit. C, 3% calcium, 4% iron

NUTMEG BEIGNETS

Enjoy these hot, yeasty pastries the New Orleans way: with a cup of Creole coffee made from java beans blended with roasted chicory.

Prep: 40 minutes   **Chill:** 4 hours   **Stand:** 30 minutes   **Cook:** About 1 minute per batch   **Oven:** 300°F
Makes: 30 beignets

3 to 3¼ cups all-purpose flour	½ teaspoon salt
1 package active dry yeast	1 egg
1¼ teaspoons grated fresh nutmeg or 1 teaspoon ground nutmeg	Shortening or cooking oil for deep-fat frying
1 cup milk	Powdered sugar (optional)
¼ cup sugar	Honey (optional)
2 tablespoons shortening	

1 In a large bowl stir together 1½ cups of the flour, the yeast, and nutmeg. In a small saucepan heat and stir the milk, sugar, 2 tablespoons shortening, and salt just until mixture is warm (120°F to 130°F) and shortening is almost melted.

2 Add the milk mixture to the flour mixture. Add the egg. Beat the milk, flour, and egg mixture with an electric mixer on low speed for 30 seconds, scraping bowl. Beat on high speed for 3 minutes. Using a spoon, stir in enough of the remaining flour to make a soft dough.

3 Place the dough in a greased bowl; turn once to grease the surface. Cover and refrigerate the dough for 4 to 24 hours.

4 Turn dough out onto a lightly floured surface. Cover; let rest for 10 minutes. Roll into a 15×12-inch rectangle; cut into thirty 3×2-inch rectangles. Cover; let rest 20 minutes (dough will not double).

5 In a deep saucepan, heat 3 inches of shortening to 375°F. (Or use a deep fryer set to 375°F.) Fry a few dough rectangles at a time in deep hot shortening about 1 minute or until beignets are golden brown on both sides, turning once. Drain on paper towels. Keep warm in a 300° oven while cooking remaining beignets. If desired, lightly sift powdered sugar over beignets. Serve warm, drizzled with honey, if desired.

Nutrition Facts per beignet: 111 cal., 5 g total fat (1 g sat. fat), 8 mg chol., 46 mg sodium, 16 g carbo., 0 g fiber, 2 g pro.
Daily Values: 1% calcium, 3% iron

Successful deep frying requires proper oil temperature. If using a saucepan, be sure to add enough oil for a thermometer reading.

Long-handled tongs enable you to keep a safe distance from hot oil. Turn beignets halfway through cooking for even browning.

SOUTHERN PECAN PIE

Southerners love their native pecans, whether they eat them out of hand, in New Orleans' famous pralines, or in this classic pie.

Prep: 35 minutes   **Bake:** 45 minutes   **Oven:** 350°F   **Makes:** 8 servings

1¼ **cups all-purpose flour**	⅔ **cup sugar**
¼ **teaspoon salt**	⅓ **cup margarine or butter, melted**
⅓ **cup shortening**	1 **tablespoon all-purpose flour**
¼ **cup finely chopped pecans**	2 **tablespoons bourbon (optional)**
4 **to 5 tablespoons cold water**	1 **teaspoon vanilla**
3 **eggs**	1½ **cups pecan halves**
1 **cup light-colored corn syrup**	**Whipped cream**

1 For pastry, in a medium bowl stir together the 1¼ cups flour and salt. Using a pastry blender, cut shortening into flour mixture until pieces are pea-size. Stir in the ¼ cup pecans. Sprinkle 1 tablespoon of the water over part of the flour mixture; gently toss with a fork. Push moistened dough to the side of the bowl. Repeat moistening flour mixture, using 1 tablespoon of water at a time, until all the flour mixture is moistened. Form dough into a ball.

2 On a lightly floured surface, use your hands to slightly flatten dough. Roll dough from center to edges into a circle about 12 inches in diameter. To transfer pastry, wrap it around the rolling pin. Unroll pastry into a 9-inch pie plate. Ease pastry into pie plate without stretching. Trim pastry ½ inch beyond edge of pie plate. Fold under extra pastry. Make a fluted edge. Do not prick pastry.

3 For filling, in a mixing bowl lightly beat eggs with a rotary beater. Stir in corn syrup, sugar, margarine, the 1 tablespoon flour, the bourbon, and vanilla. Mix well; stir in the 1½ cups pecan halves.

4 Place pastry-lined pie plate on an oven rack. Pour the filling into the pastry-lined pie plate. To prevent overbrowning, cover edge of pie with foil. Bake at 350° for 25 minutes. Remove foil; bake for 20 to 25 minutes more or until a knife inserted near center comes out clean. Cool on a wire rack.

5 Serve with whipped cream. Cover and refrigerate any remaining pie.

Nutrition Facts per serving: 644 cal., 40 g total fat (12 g sat. fat), 122 mg chol., 233 mg sodium, 65 g carbo., 3 g fiber, 7 g pro. **Daily Values:** 13% vit. A, 1% vit. C, 5% calcium, 11% iron

SPECIAL MENU
Skillet Cornbread
Chicken, Oyster, + Sausage Gumbo
Fried Green Tomatoes
W/TARRAGON MAYONNAISE
caramelized Sweet Potatoes
Raisin Bread Pudding
W/WHISKEY SAUCE

SKILLET CORN BREAD

Crisp on the outside, moist on the inside, properly made Southern corn bread is one of life's simple pleasures. The secret is to preheat the oil and the skillet, mixing the hot oil into the batter.

Prep: 10 minutes   **Bake:** 15 minutes   **Oven:** 450°F   **Cool:** 5 minutes   **Makes:** 8 servings

2 **tablespoons cooking oil**	¼ **teaspoon baking soda**
3 **eggs**	½ **teaspoon salt**
1 **cup buttermilk or sour milk***	1½ **cups yellow cornmeal**
1½ **teaspoons baking powder**	

1 Pour cooking oil into a 9-inch cast iron skillet or a 9×1½-inch round baking pan. Place pan in oven while preheating oven to 450°.

2 Meanwhile, in a large bowl combine eggs and buttermilk with a wire whisk. Add baking powder, baking soda, and salt; stir to combine. Pour hot oil from pan into egg mixture and mix well. Stir in the cornmeal. Carefully pour batter into the hot skillet, spreading evenly.

3 Bake at 450° for 15 to 20 minutes or until a wooden toothpick inserted near center comes out clean. Cool in skillet for 5 minutes. Loosen edges. Carefully invert to remove from skillet. Turn bread brown side up and cool slightly on a wire rack. Cut into wedges to serve. Serve warm.

***Note:** To make sour milk, for each cup of sour milk needed, place 1 tablespoon lemon juice or vinegar in a glass measure. Add enough milk to make 1 cup total liquid; stir. Let the mixture stand for 5 minutes before using.

Nutrition Facts per : 165 cal., 6 g total fat (1 g sat. fat), 80 mg chol., 316 mg sodium, 21 g carbo., 2 g fiber, 5 g pro.
Daily Values: 5% vit. A, 1% vit. C, 9% calcium, 8% iron

CHICKEN, OYSTER, AND SAUSAGE GUMBO

Gumbo is a derivative of the African word for okra, one of two ingredients you can use to garnish this Cajun stew. The other ingredient is filé powder, the contribution of Choctaw Indians, who ground it from dried sassafras leaves. Purists say to use one or the other but not both.

Start to Finish: 1½ hours   **Makes:** 6 servings

⅓ cup all-purpose flour

⅓ cup cooking oil

1 large onion, chopped

½ cup chopped green sweet pepper

4 cloves garlic, minced

½ teaspoon ground black pepper

¼ teaspoon ground red pepper

4 cups hot water

1 pound skinless, boneless chicken thighs, cut into bite-size pieces

12 ounces andouille or smoked sausage, cut into ½-inch slices and halved

1 pint shucked oysters, rinsed and drained

Hot cooked rice

Whole okra, split to stem (optional)

Filé powder (optional)

1 To make a roux,* in a heavy 4-quart Dutch oven heat the ⅓ cup oil over medium heat for 5 minutes. Gradually stir or whisk in the flour until smooth. Cook over medium-low heat about 20 minutes or until the mixture is dark reddish brown (chocolate brown), stirring frequently.

2 Stir in the onion, sweet pepper, garlic, black pepper, and red pepper. Cook and stir over medium heat for 3 to 5 minutes or until vegetables are tender. Gradually stir the hot water into the vegetable mixture. Stir in the chicken. Bring the mixture to boiling; reduce heat. Simmer, covered, for 40 minutes.

3 Stir in the sausage. Simmer, covered, about 20 minutes more or until chicken is tender. Remove from heat. Skim off fat.

4 Stir oysters into gumbo. Simmer, covered, for 5 to 10 minutes or until the oysters are done and the mixture is hot.

5 Spoon the hot mixture over hot rice. If desired, garnish with okra. If desired, serve ¼ to ½ teaspoon filé powder on the side of servings to be stirred into the gumbo.

Make-ahead tip: Prepare roux; cool. Transfer to a jar or refrigerator container; cover and refrigerate for up to 24 hours before using.

*Note: A roux is a thickener for soups and stews commonly used in Creole and Cajun cooking; see page 269.

Nutrition Facts per serving: 623 cal., 36 g total fat (9 g sat. fat), 120 mg chol., 1,056 mg sodium, 34 g carbo., 3 g fiber, 38 g pro. **Daily Values:** 25% vit. C, 5% calcium, 43% iron

FRIED GREEN TOMATOES WITH TARRAGON MAYONNAISE

Because some of the oil is absorbed as the slices fry, add more oil to the skillet as needed, letting the oil heat before frying the next batch of tomatoes.

Prep: 20 minutes   **Cook:** 6 minutes per batch   **Makes:** 4 servings

- ¼ cup cornmeal
- 2 tablespoons all-purpose flour
- ½ teaspoon salt
- ½ teaspoon dried thyme, crushed
- ⅛ teaspoon ground black pepper
- 2 firm green tomatoes (about 1 pound), sliced ½ inch thick
- 3 tablespoons cooking oil

- ¼ cup mayonnaise
- 2 tablespoons milk
- 2 teaspoons snipped fresh tarragon
- 1 clove garlic, minced
- Fresh tarragon sprigs (optional)
- Mixed bitter greens, such as arugula, curly endive, and escarole (optional)

1 In a shallow dish combine the cornmeal, flour, salt, thyme, and pepper. Coat tomato slices with the cornmeal mixture.

2 In a 12-inch skillet cook the tomato slices in the hot oil over medium heat for 3 to 4 minutes on each side or until browned. Remove the tomato slices; drain on paper towels.

3 Meanwhile, in a small bowl combine the mayonnaise, milk, snipped tarragon, and garlic. Arrange tomato slices on a serving platter. If desired, garnish with additional fresh tarragon. Pass mayonnaise mixture.

Nutrition Facts per serving: 269 cal., 21 g total fat (3 g sat. fat), 5 mg chol., 384 mg sodium, 16 g carbo., 2 g fiber, 2 g pro. **Daily Values:** 16% vit. A, 45% vit. C, 3% calcium, 5% iron

Serving suggestion: Serve with mixed bitter greens, such as arugula, curly endive, and escarole.

263

CARAMELIZED SWEET POTATOES

The humble sweet potato is transformed into the belle of the ball when sauteed with onions and brown sugar.

Start to Finish: 30 minutes   **Makes:** 4 side-dish servings

2 large red or white onions, cut into ¾-inch pieces

4 teaspoons margarine or butter

2 large sweet potatoes, peeled and sliced ½ inch thick (about 1 pound)

¼ cup water

2 tablespoons brown sugar

¾ teaspoon snipped fresh rosemary or ¼ teaspoon dried rosemary, crushed

   Snipped fresh rosemary (optional)

1 In a large skillet cook onions in hot margarine over medium-high heat for 3 to 4 minutes or until onions are nearly tender, stirring frequently. Stir in the sweet potatoes and water. Cook, covered, over medium heat for 10 to 12 minutes or until potatoes are nearly tender when tested with a fork, stirring occasionally.

2 Add the brown sugar and the ¾ teaspoon fresh rosemary or, if using, the ¼ teaspoon dried rosemary, to skillet. Cook, stirring gently, over medium-low heat for 4 to 5 minutes or until onions and sweet potatoes are glazed. If desired, garnish with additional fresh rosemary.

264

Nutrition Facts per serving: 173 cal., 4 g total fat (1 g sat. fat), 0 mg chol., 57 mg sodium, 33 g carbo., 4 g fiber, 2 g pro.
Daily Values: 41% vit. C, 3% calcium, 4% iron

RAISIN BREAD PUDDING WITH WHISKEY SAUCE

Cajun and Creole cooks are known for their thriftiness. When they cook, nothing goes to waste. They're also known for the richness of their food. This classic from New Orleans most likely was developed as a way to use what was left of yesterday's loaves.

Prep: 15 minutes   **Bake:** 40 minutes   **Oven:** 325°F   **Makes:** 6 servings

3 **cups French bread cubes**	2 **teaspoons vanilla**
⅔ **cup sugar**	¾ **cup sugar**
¼ **cup butter**	2 **teaspoons cornstarch**
2 **eggs**	**Dash ground cinnamon or nutmeg**
1¾ **cups whipping cream**	1 **to 2 tablespoons bourbon or**
3 **tablespoons raisins**	**1 teaspoon vanilla**

1 Arrange bread cubes in a single layer in a 2-quart square or a 10×2-inch round baking dish.

2 In a medium mixing bowl beat the ⅔ cup sugar and butter with an electric mixer until creamy. Add the eggs; beat until fluffy. Stir in 1 cup of the whipping cream, raisins, and the 2 teaspoons vanilla. Pour over bread cubes.

3 Place the baking dish in a larger baking pan on an oven rack. Pour boiling water into the larger pan around the dish to a depth of 1 inch. Bake at 325° for 40 to 50 minutes or until a knife inserted near center comes out clean. Remove the baking dish from the hot water. Cool slightly.

4 Meanwhile, for sauce, in a small saucepan combine the ¾ cup sugar, the cornstarch, and cinnamon. Stir in the remaining ¾ cup whipping cream. Cook and stir over medium heat until thickened and bubbly. Cook and stir for 1 minute more. Remove from heat; stir in bourbon.

5 Serve warm bread pudding with the bourbon sauce. Cover and refrigerate any remaining sauce. Reheat sauce over low heat, stirring occasionally.

Nutrition Facts per serving: 587 cal., 36 g total fat (21 g sat. fat), 187 mg chol., 252 mg sodium, 62 g carbo., 1 g fiber, 5 g pro. **Daily Values:** 1% vit. C, 7% calcium, 5% iron

Menu

Cajun BBC Shrimp

Chicken Etouffée

CORN CAKES

CAJUN FRIED OKRA

BANANAS Foster

CAJUN BARBECUED SHRIMP

Some say Cajun dishes change with every bite—and the last bite is as good as the first. A savory mix of fresh herbs and spices ensures that this barbecued shrimp lives up to its name.

Prep: 15 minutes   **Cook:** 25 minutes   **Makes:** 8 servings

⅓ cup butter	4 teaspoons Worcestershire sauce
⅓ cup olive oil	½ teaspoon salt
8 cloves garlic, minced	1 teaspoon paprika
2 tablespoons snipped fresh basil	1½ teaspoons crushed red pepper
1 tablespoon snipped fresh rosemary	2 pounds medium unshelled shrimp*
1 cup seafood stock or chicken broth	Warm French bread slices**
2 tablespoons lemon juice	

1 In a 12-inch cast-iron or heavy skillet melt the butter. Add olive oil and garlic. Stir over medium heat for 1 minute. Add remaining ingredients, except the shrimp and bread; heat to boiling. Reduce heat. Simmer, uncovered, over low heat for 15 minutes. Add shrimp; cook and stir over medium heat until the shrimp are opaque, about 5 minutes. Transfer the shrimp and juices to a deep serving platter. Serve with warm French bread for dipping.

267

*Note: If possible, purchase deveined shrimp in shells. Cooking the shrimp in the shells intensifies the flavor.

**Note: Wrap sliced French bread in foil and heat in a 350°F oven about 15 minutes.

Nutrition Facts per serving: 255 cal., 18 g total fat (6 g sat. fat), 151 mg chol., 432 mg sodium, 3 g carbo., 0 g fiber, 18 g pro. **Daily Values:** 13% vit. A, 8% vit. C, 6% calcium, 14% iron

CHICKEN ÉTOUFFÉE

Ask Cajun or Creole cooks how to make a favorite recipe, and they'll likely tell you to make a roux first. The rich flavor of étouffée, gumbo, and other authentic southern Louisiana sauces and stews relies on this mixture of cooked fat and flour.

Prep: 20 minutes **Cook:** 55 minutes **Makes:** 5 or 6 servings

⅓ cup cooking oil	¼ cup snipped fresh parsley
⅓ cup all-purpose flour	1 tablespoon minced garlic (6 cloves)
2 cups chopped onions (4 medium)	1 14-ounce can chicken broth
1 cup chopped celery (2 stalks)	1 pound skinless, boneless chicken, cubed
½ cup chopped green sweet pepper	1 teaspoon seasoned salt
1 tablespoon cooking oil	1 bay leaf
¼ cup sliced green onions	Hot cooked rice

1 To make a roux, in a large skillet heat the ⅓ cup oil over medium heat for 5 minutes. Gradually stir or whisk in the flour until smooth. Cook over medium-low heat about 20 minutes or until the mixture is dark reddish brown (chocolate brown), stirring frequently.

2 Meanwhile, in a large saucepan or Dutch oven cook the onions, celery, and sweet pepper in the 1 tablespoon oil over medium heat for 10 minutes, stirring occasionally. Stir in the roux, green onions, parsley, and garlic. Add chicken broth all at once, stirring to combine. Stir in the chicken, seasoned salt, and bay leaf.

3 Bring to boiling; reduce heat. Simmer, covered, about 20 minutes or until chicken is tender and no longer pink, stirring frequently. Discard bay leaf. Serve over rice.

Nutrition Facts per serving: 461 cal., 21 g total fat (3 g sat. fat), 63 mg chol., 731 mg sodium, 42 g carbo., 2 g fiber, 25 g pro. **Daily Values:** 7% vit. A, 41% vit. C, 7% calcium, 18% iron

269

The oil should be hot before slowly and gradually stirring in the flour. This helps avoid lumps.

It takes a lot of stirring and waiting to make a good, dark roux. The finished color is a coppery, dark brown.

CORN CAKES

Supper in Louisiana often consists of fresh in-season greens fried with bacon and a wedge of warm corn bread. These herbed corn cakes are a tasty take on that tradition, and they're elegant enough to serve as a side dish when company comes for dinner.

Start to Finish: 30 minutes   **Makes:** 6 side-dish servings

- 1 fresh ear of corn or ½ cup frozen whole kernel corn
- 2 tablespoons all-purpose flour
- 1½ teaspoons baking powder
- 1 teaspoon sugar
- ½ teaspoon salt
- 1 cup boiling water
- 1 cup yellow cornmeal

- ¼ cup milk
- 1 egg, slightly beaten
- 1 tablespoon snipped fresh chives
- 3 tablespoons cooking oil
- 1 teaspoon snipped fresh chives or cilantro (optional)
- ⅓ cup dairy sour cream

1 Cut corn kernels from cob and measure ½ cup. In a small bowl combine flour, baking powder, sugar, and salt. Set aside.

2 In a medium bowl stir boiling water into cornmeal to make a stiff mush. Stir in milk until smooth. Stir in corn, egg, and the 1 tablespoon chives. Add flour mixture to corn mixture and stir just until combined.

3 In a large skillet heat 2 tablespoons of the oil over medium heat. Drop batter by rounded tablespoons into 2 tablespoons of hot oil. Cook for 3 to 4 minutes or until golden brown, turning once. Transfer to a serving platter; cover and keep warm. Add the remaining oil and repeat with remaining batter.

4 If desired, stir the 1 teaspoon chives into the sour cream. Serve sour cream with the corn cakes.

Nutrition Facts per serving: 215 cal., 11 g total fat (3 g sat. fat), 42 mg chol., 295 mg sodium, 25 g carbo., 2 g fiber, 4 g pro. **Daily Values:** 2% vit. C, 10% calcium, 9% iron

CAJUN FRIED OKRA

Keep the crisp coins of fried okra warm in a 300°F oven while you fry the remaining batches.

Prep: 15 minutes   **Cook:** 3 minutes per batch   **Makes:** 4 servings

- ⅓ cup all-purpose flour
- ⅓ cup yellow cornmeal
- 1 tablespoon Cajun seasoning
- 1 egg, slightly beaten
- 1 tablespoon milk

- ½ pound whole okra, cut into ½-inch pieces (2 cups)
- Cooking oil or shortening for deep-fat frying
- Salsa (optional)

1 In a plastic bag combine flour, cornmeal, and Cajun seasoning. In a small bowl combine egg and milk. Toss okra pieces in egg mixture. Add one-fourth of the okra to the plastic bag; close bag and shake to coat okra well. Remove coated okra. Repeat with remaining okra.

2 In a large skillet heat ¼ inch oil. Fry okra, one-fourth at a time, over medium-high heat for 3 to 4 minutes or until golden brown, turning once. Remove from oil; drain on paper towels. Serve warm, with salsa, if desired.

Nutrition Facts per serving: 370 cal., 29 g total fat (5 g sat. fat), 54 mg chol., 160 mg sodium, 24 g carbo., 2 g fiber, 5 g pro. **Daily Values:** 22% vit. C, 6% calcium, 12% iron

BANANAS FOSTER

During the 1950s, chefs at Brennan's Restaurant in New Orleans named this quick and showy dessert for Richard Foster, one of their regular customers.

Start to Finish: 15 minutes   **Makes:** 4 servings

⅓ **cup butter**

⅓ **cup packed brown sugar**

2 **tablespoons crème de cacao or banana liqueur**

3 **ripe bananas, bias-sliced (2 cups)**

¼ **teaspoon ground cinnamon**

¼ **cup rum**

2 **cups vanilla ice cream**

1 In a large skillet melt butter; stir in brown sugar until melted. Stir in crème de cacao. Add bananas; cook and gently stir over medium heat about 2 minutes or until heated through. Sprinkle with cinnamon.

2 In a saucepan heat rum until it almost simmers. Ignite rum with a very long match. Pour over bananas; stir gently to coat. Spoon sauce over ice cream; serve immediately.

Nutrition Facts per serving: 483 cal., 24 g total fat (15 g sat. fat), 72 mg chol., 225 mg sodium, 57 g carbo., 2 g fiber, 3 g pro. **Daily Values:** 19% vit. A, 14% vit. C, 11% calcium, 4% iron

GLOSSARY
of ingredients and terms

A

Adobo sauce A dark-red Mexican sauce made from ground chiles, herbs, and vinegar. Chipotle chile peppers are often sold packed in cans of adobo sauce.

Al dente (al-DEN-tay) Italian for "to the tooth." It describes pasta that is cooked until it offers a slight resistance when bitten into, rather than cooked until soft.

Anaheim A light to medium green chile that is long and narrow. It has a sweet, slightly spicy flavor that makes it wonderful stuffed and cooked or raw in salsas and salads.

Ancho (AHN-choh) A dried poblano pepper. It is 3 to 4 inches long with a deep reddish color. Its flavor is sweet and fruity and ranges from mild to hot.

Andouille sausage is a spicy Cajun pork sausage available at specialty stores. If you cannot find it, substitute Polish kielbasa and ¼ teaspoon red pepper flakes.

Arborio rice A short grain Italian variety that is ideal for risotto because it tends to produce a creamy texture as it is slowly cooked and stirred.

Arugula (ah-ROO-guh-lah) A salad green with a slightly bitter, peppery mustard flavor. It is also known as rocket, rucola, and roquette.

Asadero A Mexican variety of cow's-milk cheese that is sometimes shaped in braids or balls. It is a good melting cheese for Mexican cooking.

Asafetida Used in many Indian dishes, this seasoning has a somewhat unpleasant aroma before cooking (hence its name, derived from the Latin word "foetida"—smelly or rotten!), but when cooked produces an onion and garlic flavor. It substitutes for onions in cultures that are not allowed to eat them.

B

Balsamic vinegar Made from white Trebbiano grape juice, balsamic vinegar gets its distinctive brown color, syrupy body, and slight sweetness from being aged for years in barrels.

Basmati rice An aromatic, long grain brown or white rice from India and California. Indian types are often aged to intensify the flavor. Containing a very small amount of a sticky type of starch, basmati is nutty and fluffy.

C

Cajun seasoning While the blends available may differ, most are peppery hot. They can include onion, garlic, and salt with the classic Cajun trio of white, black, and red peppers.

Chayote (shi-OH-tay) A green, mild-flavored, pear-shaped fruit that has been used in Mexican cooking for centuries. It is usually cooked, but can be eaten raw. Chayote can be found in Mexican markets.

Chili sauce Used as a condiment in some types of Asian cooking, chili sauce usually contains chile peppers or powder, tomatoes, onions, green sweet peppers, vinegar, sugar, and other spices.

Chipotle (chih-POHT-lay) A smoked, dried jalapeño chile pepper. Chipotles have wrinkly brown skin and a rich, smoky flavor. They can be found dried or canned in adobo sauce. See *adobo sauce*.

Chutney A condiment often used in Indian cuisine that's made of chopped fruit, vegetables, and spices enlivened by hot chile peppers, fresh ginger, or vinegar.

Clarified butter Butter that has had the milk solids removed. Clarified butter can be heated to high temperatures without burning. See *ghee*.

Coconut milk A product made from water and coconut pulp that's often used in Southeast Asian and Indian cooking. Coconut milk is not the clear liquid in the center of the coconut, nor should it be confused with cream of coconut, a sweetened concoction often used to make mixed drinks.

Couscous (KOOS-koos) A granular pasta popular in North Africa that's made from semolina. Look for it in the rice and pasta section of supermarkets.

Curry paste A blend of herbs, spices, and hot chile peppers that's often used in Thai and Indian cooking. Look for it in Asian markets and large supermarkets. Curry pastes are available in many varieties and are sometimes classified by color (green, red, or yellow), by heat (mild or hot), or by a particular style of curry dish (such as Panang or Masaman).

F

Fava bean A tan, flat bean that looks like a large lima bean. It is available dried, canned, and, occasionally, fresh.

Filé A powder made from dried sassafras leaves, it is also called filé powder or gumbo filé. It is a traditional flavoring and thickening agent in Creole cooking.

Fish sauce A pungent brown sauce made by fermenting fish, usually anchovies, in brine. It's often used in Southeast Asian cooking.

Five-spice powder Combinations may vary, but this fragrant Asian seasoning blend usually includes cinnamon, anise seeds or star anise, fennel, black or Szechwan pepper, and cloves.

G

Garam masala Traditionally thought to warm the body, garam masala simply means "hot spices." It originated in cold northern India and is a variable mix of spices that often includes cloves, cinnamon, bay leaf, black pepper, nutmeg, mace, and cardamom. It can be found in Indian markets and some large supermarkets.

Ghee (GEE) An Indian version of clarified butter which is available in specialty markets. See *clarified butter*.

Ginger The rootlike rhizomes of a semitropical plant that adds a spicy-sweet flavor to recipes of several cuisines, most notably Asian. It should be peeled before use.

Ginger, crystallized A confection made from pieces of ginger cooked in a sugar syrup, then coated with sugar. Also known as candied ginger.

Gumbo The word "gumbo" is from an African word meaning "okra." This Creole stew contains okra, tomatoes, and onions, as well as various meats or shellfish such as shrimp, chicken, or sausage. It is thickened with a roux. See *roux*.

H

Habañero Among the hottest of all chile peppers, habañeros are small and look like little lanterns. They range in color from light green to red-orange.

Hoisin sauce A sauce, popular in Asian cooking (most notably Chinese), that brings a multitude of sweet and spicy flavors to a dish: fermented soybeans, molasses, vinegar, mustard, sesame seeds, garlic, and chile peppers. Look for hoisin near the soy sauce in large supermarkets or Asian markets.

J

Jamaican jerk A spice mix of varying ingredients that originated on the island of Jamaica. It often includes allspice, thyme, cinnamon, ginger, cloves, onion, garlic, and ground chiles.

Jasmine rice A fragrant, long grain variety of rice from Thailand and Vietnam.

Jicama (HEE-kah-mah) A large, bulbous root vegetable with tan skin and white crunchy flesh. The skin is easily peeled, and the sweet flesh can be eaten raw or cooked. Popular in Mexican cooking.

K

Kosher salt A coarse salt with no additives that many cooks prefer for its light, flaky texture and clean taste. It also has a lower sodium content than regular salt.

L

Lard A product made from pork fat that is sometimes used for baking and in tamales, in which it helps provide light texture and characteristic flavor.

Lemongrass A highly aromatic, lemon-flavored herb often used in several types of Asian cooking. To use, trim the fibrous ends and slice what remains into 3- to 4-inch sections. Cut each section in half, lengthwise, exposing the layers. Rinse pieces under cold water to remove any grit and slice the lemongrass thinly.

M

Mascarpone (mas-kar-POHN) An extremely rich Italian type of cow's-milk cheese that is popular in desserts.

Matzo A thin, unleavened bread eaten by Jews at Passover, because it contains the only type of flour that is allowed at that time.

Mithai This term describes a number of Eastern Indian sweets, including halvai and barfi, which are available at Indian markets or through mail order.

O

Oyster sauce A popular Asian condiment and seasoning made with oysters, brine, and soy sauce. This concentrated brown sauce has a rich flavor but is not overpowering.

P

Pancetta (pan-CHEH-tuh) Italian-style bacon that's made from the belly (pancia) of a hog; unlike bacon, pancetta is not smoked, but instead seasoned with pepper and other spices and cured with salt. Pancetta is generally available packaged in a sausagelike roll.

Pappadums An extremely thin type of bread from India that is most often made from chickpea flour. They cook up with a bubbly, crisp texture, and many varieties are highly seasoned, often spicy hot. They can be purchased in unbaked form in Indian markets and can be fried in hot oil, baked in the oven on a baking sheet or stone, or even cooked over an open flame. They cook extremely rapidly by almost any method.

Pesto Traditionally an uncooked sauce made from crushed garlic, basil, and nuts blended with Parmesan cheese and olive oil. Modern pestos often incorporate other herbs or greens.

Phyllo (FEE-loh) Prominent in Greek, Turkish, and Near Eastern dishes, phyllo consists of tissue-thin sheets of dough that, when layered and baked, results in a delicate, flaky pastry. The word "phyllo" (sometimes spelled filo) is Greek for "leaf." Although phyllo can be made at home, a frozen commercial product is available and much handier to use.

Plum sauce A Chinese condiment sometimes referred to as duck sauce, this thick sauce is usually made from plums, apricots, sugar, and spices.

Poblano (poh-BLAH-noh) A blackish green chile pepper with a flavor that ranges from mild to quite spicy.

Polenta (poh-LEHN-tah) Italian for "cornmeal mush." This mush can be eaten hot or spread out and cooled until firm. The cooled polenta is then cut and fried or broiled.

Poori A deep-fried Indian flatbread that puffs when cooked. (The plural form of the word is "pooris.") See the recipe, page 174.

Prosciutto (proh-SHOO-toh) A type of ham that has been seasoned, salt-cured, and air-dried (rather than smoked). The process takes at least nine months and results in somewhat sweetly spiced, rose-colored meats with a sheen.

R

Rice papers These round, flat, edible papers, made from the pith of a rice-paper plant, are used for wrapping spring rolls.

Rice vinegar A mild-flavored vinegar made from fermented sticky rice. Rice vinegar is interchangeable with rice wine vinegar, which is made from fermented rice wine. Seasoned rice vinegar, with added sugar and salt, can be used in recipes calling for rice vinegar, though you may wish to adjust the seasonings.

Roux (roo) A French term that refers to a mixture of flour and a fat cooked to a range of colors from golden to rich coppery brown. Roux is used as a thickening and flavoring agent in sauces, soups, and gumbos.

S

Schmaltz A Jewish term for rendered chicken fat used in cooking. See page 238 for how to make it.

Scotch bonnet A small fiery chile pepper that ranges from yellow to red in color. Popular in island cooking, it is closely related to the habañero and is as hot.

Shrimp paste A pungent seasoning made from dried, salted shrimp that has been pounded into a paste. Shrimp paste gives Southeast Asian dishes an authentic, rich flavor.

Soba noodles Made from wheat and buckwheat flours, soba noodles are a favorite Japanese fast food.

Somen noodles Made from wheat flour, these dried Japanese noodles are very fine and most often white.

Sticky rice Also known as glutinous rice, this variety has a very high amount of amylopectin, a type of starch that causes it to stick strongly together. This type of rice is popular in desserts or Chinese dishes that include shaped rice.

T

Tahini A flavoring agent, often used in Middle Eastern cooking, made from ground sesame seeds. Look for tahini in specialty food shops, Asian markets, or large supermarkets.

Tofu Also known as bean curd, tofu is made by curdling soy milk in a process similar to cheesemaking. Although it is almost tasteless by itself, tofu acts as a sponge, easily absorbing other flavors. The most dense varieties are known as extra-firm or firm, not to be confused with a softer variety called silken tofu, which also includes extra-firm and firm varieties. A variety called soft tofu is ideal for whipping, blending, or crumbling for use in dressings, dips, and desserts.

Turmeric This important ingredient of Indian curry powder is bright yellowish orange and has an earthy, bitter flavor.

U

Udon (oo-DOHN) A thick Japanese type of noodle that can be made from wheat or corn flour.

W

Wontons, wonton wrappers Stuffed, usually savory, Asian pastries. (But see Banana Wontons, page 55.) The wrappers, paper-thin skins used to make wontons, can be found in the produce aisle or in Asian markets. Wonton wrappers are similar to, but smaller than, egg roll skins.

RESOURCES
Internet and Mail Order Resources for Ethnic Food and Ingredients

GENERAL ETHNIC INGREDIENTS:

www.theglobalgrocery.com
Phone (615) 321-1331
Fax (615) 321-1631

www.ethnicgrocer.com
Phone (866) 4ETHNIC (1-866-438-4642)

www.igourmet.com
Phone (877) IGOURMET

Earthy Delights
www.earthy.com
Phone (800) 367-4709 or (517) 668-2402
Fax (517) 668-1213

The CMC Company
www.thecmccompany.com
Phone (800) CMC-2780

ASIAN:

www.asiafoods.com
Phone (877) 902-0841

www.importfood.com
Phone (888) 618-THAI (8424)
 or (425) 392-7516
Fax (425) 391-5658

www.thaigrocer.com
Phone (773) 988-8424
Fax (773) 871-3969

www.orientalpantry.com
Phone (978) 264-4576
Fax (781) 275-4506

CAJUN AND CREOLE:

www.cajungrocer.com
Fax (337) 264-1366
Phone (888) 272-9347

www.cajun-shop.com
Phone (225) 751-8112

www.neworleansoriginals.com
Phone (888) 464-4982

CARIBBEAN:

www.caribshop.com
Phone (800) 563-1747
Fax (630) 839-5864

INDIAN:

www.namaste.com
Phone (847) 640-1105

www.indiaplaza.com
Phone (408) 345-3900 or (877) Y2-INDIA
Fax (408) 345-3963

ITALIAN:

www.salami.com
Phone (516) 872-3450
Fax (516) 872-1706

www.fromitalia.com
(866) 648-2542

www.flyingnoodle.com
Phone (800) 566-0599 or 781-829-6879
Fax (781) 829-9317

www.pastacheese.com
Phone (800) 386-9198

MEXICAN:

www.mex-grocer.com
Phone (858) 459-0577
Fax (858) 459-0595

INDEX

279

286

METRIC INFORMATION

The charts on this page provide a guide for converting measurements from the U.S. customary system, which is used throughout this book, to the metric system.

Product Differences

Most of the ingredients called for in the recipes in this book are available in most countries. However, some are known by different names. Here are some common American ingredients and their possible counterparts:

- Sugar (white) is granulated, fine granulated, or castor sugar.
- Powdered sugar is icing sugar.
- All-purpose flour is enriched, bleached or unbleached white household flour. When self-rising flour is used in place of all-purpose flour in a recipe that calls for leavening, omit the leavening agent (baking soda or baking powder) and salt.
- Light-colored corn syrup is golden syrup.
- Cornstarch is cornflour.
- Baking soda is bicarbonate of soda.
- Vanilla or vanilla extract is vanilla essence.
- Green, red, or yellow sweet peppers are capsicums or bell peppers.
- Golden raisins are sultanas.

Volume and Weight

The United States traditionally uses cup measures for liquid and solid ingredients. The chart below shows the approximate imperial and metric equivalents. If you are accustomed to weighing solid ingredients, the following approximate equivalents will be helpful.

- 1 cup butter, castor sugar, or rice = 8 ounces = 1/2 pound = 250 grams
- 1 cup flour = 4 ounces = 1/4 pound = 125 grams
- 1 cup icing sugar = 5 ounces = 150 grams

Canadian and U.S. volume for a cup measure is 8 fluid ounces (237 ml), but the standard metric equivalent is 250 ml.

1 British imperial cup is 10 fluid ounces.

In Australia, 1 tablespoon equals 20 ml, and there are 4 teaspoons in the Australian tablespoon.

Spoon measures are used for smaller amounts of ingredients. Although the size of the tablespoon varies slightly in different countries, for practical purposes and for recipes in this book, a straight substitution is all that's necessary. Measurements made using cups or spoons always should be level unless stated otherwise.

Common Weight Range Replacements

Imperial / U.S.	Metric
1/2 ounce	15 g
1 ounce	25 g or 30 g
4 ounces (1/4 pound)	115 g or 125 g
8 ounces (1/2 pound)	225 g or 250 g
16 ounces (1 pound)	450 g or 500 g
1 1/4 pounds	625 g
1 1/2 pounds	750 g
2 pounds or 2 1/4 pounds	1,000 g or 1 Kg

Oven Temperature Equivalents

Fahrenheit Setting	Celsius Setting*	Gas Setting
300°F	150°C	Gas Mark 2 (very low)
325°F	160°C	Gas Mark 3 (low)
350°F	180°C	Gas Mark 4 (moderate)
375°F	190°C	Gas Mark 5 (moderate)
400°F	200°C	Gas Mark 6 (hot)
425°F	220°C	Gas Mark 7 (hot)
450°F	230°C	Gas Mark 8 (very hot)
475°F	240°C	Gas Mark 9 (very hot)
500°F	260°C	Gas Mark 10 (extremely hot)
Broil	Broil	Grill

*Electric and gas ovens may be calibrated using celsius. However, for an electric oven, increase celsius setting 10 to 20 degrees when cooking above 160°C. For convection or forced air ovens (gas or electric) lower the temperature setting 25°F/10°C when cooking at all heat levels.

Baking Pan Sizes

Imperial / U.S.	Metric
9×1 1/2-inch round cake pan	22- or 23×4-cm (1.5 L)
9×1 1/2-inch pie plate	22- or 23×4-cm (1 L)
8×8×2-inch square cake pan	20×5-cm (2 L)
9×9×2-inch square cake pan	22- or 23×4.5-cm (2.5 L)
11×7×1 1/2-inch baking pan	28×17×4-cm (2 L)
2-quart rectangular baking pan	30×19×4.5-cm (3 L)
13×9×2-inch baking pan	34×22×4.5-cm (3.5 L)
15×10×1-inch jelly roll pan	40×25×2-cm
9×5×3-inch loaf pan	23×13×8-cm (2 L)
2-quart casserole	2 L

U.S. / Standard Metric Equivalents

1/8 teaspoon = 0.5 ml	
1/4 teaspoon = 1 ml	
1/2 teaspoon = 2 ml	
1 teaspoon = 5 ml	
1 tablespoon = 15 ml	
2 tablespoons = 25 ml	
1/4 cup = 2 fluid ounces = 50 ml	
1/3 cup = 3 fluid ounces = 75 ml	
1/2 cup = 4 fluid ounces = 125 ml	
2/3 cup = 5 fluid ounces = 150 ml	
3/4 cup = 6 fluid ounces = 175 ml	
1 cup = 8 fluid ounces = 250 ml	
2 cups = 1 pint = 500 ml	
1 quart = 1 litre